# The Napoleonic Wars:

## Defeat of the Grand Army

Titles in the History's Great Defeats series include:

# The Napoleonic Wars:

## Defeat of the Grand Army

by Thomas Streissguth

LUCENT
BOOKS®

THOMSON
————*————™
GALE

San Diego • Detroit • New York • San Francisco • Cleveland • New Haven, Conn. • Waterville, Maine • London • Munich

### LIBRARY OF CONGRESS CATALOGING-IN-PUBLICATION DATA

Streissguth, Thomas, 1958–
    The Napoleonic Wars: defeat of the Grand Army / by Thomas Streissguth.
    p. cm. — (History's great defeats)
    Summary: Provides a look at how Napoleon Bonaparte's egotism, unrealistic dreams,
and tendency to underestimate enemies led to the downfall of his Grande Armée during the Napoleonic Wars.
    Includes bibliographical references and index.
      ISBN 1-59018-065-8 (alk. paper)
     1. France. Armée. *Grande Armée*—History—Juvenile literature. 2. France—History,
Military—1789–1815—Juvenile Literature. 3. Napoleon I, Emperor of the French,
1769–1821—Juvenile Literature. [1. France. Army. *Grande Armée*—History. 2. Napoleon
I, Emperor of the French, 1769–1821. 3. Napoleonic Wars, 1800–1815—Campaigns. 4.
France—History, Military—1789–1815.] I. Title. II. History's great defeats
     DC202.1 .S77 2003
     940.2'74—dc21

                                                  2002151712

Printed in the United States of America

# Table of Contents

# Foreword

HISTORY IS FILLED with tales of dramatic encounters that sealed the fates of empires or civilizations, changing them or causing them to disappear forever. One of the best known events began in 334 B.C., when Alexander, king of Macedonia, led his small but formidable Greek army into Asia. In the short span of only ten years, he brought Persia, the largest empire the world had yet seen, to its knees, earning him the nickname forever after associated with his name—"the Great." The demise of Persia, which at its height stretched from the shores of the Mediterranean Sea in the west to the borders of India in the east, was one of history's most stunning defeats. It occurred primarily because of some fatal flaws in the Persian military system, disadvantages the Greeks had exploited before, though never as spectacularly as they did under Alexander.

First, though the Persians had managed to conquer many peoples and bring huge territories under their control, they had failed to create an individual fighting man who could compare with the Greek hoplite. A heavily armored infantry soldier, the hoplite fought in a highly effective and lethal battlefield formation—the phalanx. Possessed of better armor, weapons, and training than the Persians, Alexander's soldiers repeatedly crushed their Persian opponents. Second, the Persians for the most part lacked generals of the caliber of their Greek counterparts. And when Alexander invaded, Persia had the added and decisive disadvantage of facing one of the greatest generals of all time. When the Persians were defeated, their great empire was lost forever.

Other world powers and civilizations have fallen in a like manner. They have succumbed to some combination of inherent fatal flaws or disadvantages, to political and/or military mistakes, and even to the personal failings of their leaders.

Another of history's great defeats was the sad demise of the North American Indian tribes at the hands of encroaching European civilization from the sixteenth to nineteenth centuries. In this case, all of the tribes suffered from the same crippling disadvantages. Among the worst, they lacked the great numbers, the unity, and the advanced industrial and military hardware possessed by the Europeans. Still another example, one closer to our own time, was the resounding defeat of Nazi Germany by the Allies in 1945, which brought World War II, the most disastrous conflict in history, to a close. Nazi Germany collapsed for many reasons. But one of the most telling was that its leader, Adolf Hitler, sorely underestimated the material resources and human resolve of the Allies, especially the United States. In the end, Germany was in a very real sense submerged by a massive and seemingly relentless tidal wave of Allied bombs, tanks, ships, and soldiers.

Seen in retrospect, a good many of the fatal flaws, drawbacks, and mistakes that caused these and other great defeats from the pages of history seem obvious. It is only natural to wonder why, in each case, the losers did not realize their limitations and/or errors sooner and attempt to avert disaster. But closer examination of the events, social and political trends, and leading personalities involved usually reveals that complex factors were at play. Arrogance, fear, ignorance, stubbornness, innocence, and other attitudes held by nations, peoples, and individuals often colored and shaped their reactions, goals, and strategies. And it is both fascinating and instructive to reconstruct how such attitudes, as well as the fatal flaws and mistakes themselves, contributed to the losers' ultimate demise.

Each volume in Lucent Books' *History's Great Defeats* series is designed to provide the reader with diverse learning tools for exploring the topic at hand. Each well-informed, clearly written text is supported and enlivened by substantial quotes by the actual people involved, as well as by later historians and other experts; and these primary and secondary sources are carefully documented. Each volume also supplies the reader with an extensive Works Consulted list, guiding him or her to further research on the topic. These and other research tools, including glossaries and time lines, afford the reader a thorough understanding of how and why one of history's most decisive defeats occurred and how these events shaped our world.

# The Rise and Fall of the First Empire

IN THE CITY of PARIS, on December 2, 1804, an enormous procession of military leaders, police officials, politicians, courtiers, and ordinary French men and women filed across the bridges of the Seine River and assembled on the square before the cathedral of Notre Dame. Here, in the heart of the capital of France, an extraordinary man who had been born into a rather ordinary family would crown himself as the emperor of the French.

The coronation of Napoleon Bonaparte and the establishment of what historians would one day call the First Empire marked the summit of a brilliant military career. Trained as an artillery officer, Napoleon had first made his name with a skillfully led bombardment that freed the port of Toulon from occupation by naval forces of Spain and the British Empire. In the years that followed, Napoleon showed an uncanny grasp of battlefield tactics and an unerring ability to inspire the officers and troops under him. He won important victories in northern Italy in the late 1790s, a time when France, which had endured a violent, chaotic revolution, was fighting powerful European monarchies determined to destroy the nation's republican government and return France to rule by its monarchy. Largely thanks to Napoleon's military prowess, these counterrevolutionary efforts failed.

Napoleon rebuilt France's military power and international prestige—even as he was laying the groundwork for his own grandiose schemes. A campaign he led against Austria ended in the Treaty of Campo Formio, which extended French sovereignty into the wealthy, industrialized region of northern Italy. Ambitious and calculating, Napoleon then drew on his victories to attain the position of first consul, the most powerful post in the government. In 1799, at the age of thirty, he would overthrow the French government and establish himself as the country's dictator.

Driving Napoleon's ascent was the most crucial ingredient of the successful military leader: He was confident, and he imparted that confidence to his troops and to fellow officers. Napoleon never doubted himself or his goals. He always believed that his opponents within the country, his adversaries on the battlefield, and his rivals in the other states of Europe could never match him or defeat his creation, the *Grande Armée*, the "Great Army" of France.

In his ambition and self-confidence, however, lay the seeds of Napoleon's defeat. He saw everyone around him—no matter their experience or proven ability—as inferior to himself in talent, intelligence, and energy. His early victories on the battlefield made him blindly contemptuous of those who would oppose him. Napoleon

*A brilliant military strategist and unwavering egotist, Napoleon Bonaparte poses for a portrait by painter Jacques-Louis David in 1805.*

never believed that the armies of Austria or Prussia could defeat him. He did not believe that England, a nation dependent on foreign trade, could stand up to an economic blockade of Europe. He did not believe that the peasants and commoners of Spain could resist rule by imperial France. Nor did he believe that Russia, even with its vast distances and brutal winter climate, could turn back to an invasion by the *Grande Armée*. Convinced of his own invincibility, Napoleon was always ready to gamble, to strive for yet another conquest, even when he had everything to lose and little to gain by doing so.

The rise and fall of Napoleon ranks as one of the nineteenth century's most important events. Napoleon's reign fostered a new nationalism that a century after his defeat at Waterloo would result in another continent-wide war, the conflict known as World War I. In turn, World War I shaped twentieth-century Europe, and in many ways the life of Napoleon still echoes in the twenty-first century and within the continent of which he was, for a brief time, the undisputed master.

# The Failed Egyptian Campaign

**Chapter 1**

N APOLEON'S EARLY YEARS were marked by rapid advancement. Yet going hand in hand with the obvious talent that underlay that success was a character flaw that would in the end help to destroy Napoleon. The man who would one day be emperor would take no advice, heed no warnings.

## Opportunity at Toulon

December 1793 was a grim time for the people of France. The enemies of the French king Louis XVI had overthrown and then beheaded the monarch and his wife, Marie-Antoinette. The revolutionaries had established a republic in place of the monarchy, but they faced determined opponents, both at home and abroad. Royalists controlled the French port of Toulon and had surrendered it to the naval forces of England and Spain as part of a grand plan to strike back at France's revolutionary armies and restore the monarchy to power.

To prevent this from happening, the French revolutionary leaders turned to a young artillery officer, Napoleon Bonaparte, to capture Toulon. Their plans fit nicely with Napoleon's own. Ambitious and energetic, Napoleon was a fervent revolutionary—but only because he believed that the weakness of the revolutionary government presented an opportunity for his own quick advancement. To bring himself into the limelight, he was seeking a chance for a spectacular military victory.

That opportunity came in Toulon, where Napoleon positioned several batteries of artillery on the heights overlooking the port. On December 17, he unleashed a furious bombardment on the ships in the

11

*Napoleon (pictured standing) explains his battle strategy to regain control of Toulon and repel the English and Spanish fleets.*

harbor. In concert with an attack by the French infantry, this assault forced the English and Spanish to abandon Toulon.

The victory earned Napoleon a promotion to the rank of brigadier general. The republic's leaders also appointed him commander of artillery for the French forces then fighting in northern Italy, where

France was contesting control of the region with the Austrian Empire. Napoleon's great skill in handling both artillery and men brought him another promotion in 1796, to the position of overall commander of the French army in Italy. With great energy and resourcefulness, Napoleon routed the Austrians in several battles. The decisive victory came at Lodi, in the plains of the northern Italian region of Lombardy, on May 10. Five days later, Napoleon and the French army marched unopposed into Milan, Lombardy's capital.

Napoleon was quickly rising above his brother officers in the opinion of the army, of the French nation, and of himself. Years later he would recall, "It was only after [the Battle of] Lodi that I realised I was a superior being and conceived the ambition of performing great things, which hitherto had filled my thoughts only as a fantastic dream."[1]

Napoleon was a military man, but he already saw himself as something of a king. He also saw himself as superior to others; he surrounded himself with obedient staff officers and stood for no questioning of his decisions. Although he had once fostered an image as a man of the people, his personal style was changing as well. The diplomat Count Miot de Melito recalled an encounter with Napoleon during the Italian campaign at the town of Montebello on June 1, 1797:

> I was received by Buonaparte at the magnificent residence . . .
> in the midst of a brilliant court, rather than the usual army
> headquarters I had expected. . . . Strict etiquette already
> reigned round him. Even his aides-de-camp and officers were
> no longer received at his table, for he had become fastidious in
> the choice of guests whom he admitted to it. . . . He was in no
> wise embarrassed or confused by these excessive honours, but
> received them as though he had been accustomed to them all
> his life.[2]

Napoleon already saw himself as the best hope for France. He believed the time was ripe in France for a man of his abilities and cunning, and he also believed that his brilliance on the battlefield could translate into success in politics. All he needed to do, in his opinion, was to apply military strategy to politics. To prepare the ground for this success, he needed a spectacular achievement that would bring him the acclaim of the entire nation.

*Napoleon flaunts a French emperor's regalia despite rapidly climbing the ranks from his artillery officer's post.*

## The Egyptian Campaign

To gain a victory that would assure his popularity and advancement in France, Napoleon turned to Egypt. This ancient land presented a tempting target. Since 1517, Egypt had been a province of the Ottoman (Turkish) Empire, and had been ruled for the Turks by a clan known as the Mamelukes. The Mamelukes commanded a strong, skilled cavalry, but Napoleon saw this force as a disorganized rabble that would put up a weak fight against any well-planned French invasion. He took assurance from the French artillery, which he believed would easily terrify and rout the Mameluke horsemen.

A French takeover of Egypt would, Napoleon thought, serve both his and France's interests. Napoleon assumed the Egyptians would welcome French rule and French political ideals, and he believed that creating a new Egyptian republic, modeled on that of revolutionary France, would bring him acclaim among the Egyptians as well as the French. With Egypt as a French colony, France would establish itself as a power in the Middle East. The French navy and army would occupy the eastern Mediterranean and then western Asia. This would threaten English control of trade with Asia—trade that English companies and factories depended on—and force the English to recognize the French republic.

Napoleon saw England, and not Austria, Prussia, or Russia, as France's most threatening enemy, and challenging England was a vital part of his long-term strategy. As he announced to his ministers before the Egyptian campaign:

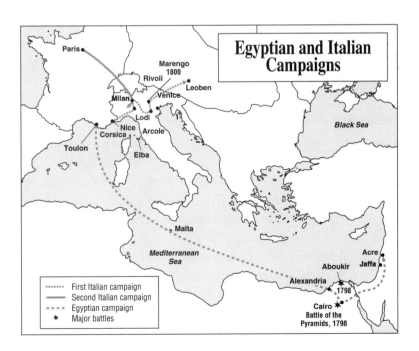

The Austrians are a clumsy and grasping nation; no state is less subtle and less likely to be a threat to our internal affairs. On the other hand, the English are courageous, meddling and energetic. We must pull down the English monarchy. . . . Let us concentrate our efforts on building up our fleet and on destroying England. Once that is done Europe is at our feet.[3]

For their part, the five directors, or leaders, of the French revolutionary government worried less about England and more about threats to their own power within France. They particularly worried about the threat posed by the popular, strong-willed Napoleon Bonaparte. They believed that the further Napoleon sailed from home, the safer they and their government would be. France was still in turmoil, and an ambitious military man, they knew, might take advantage of the troubled times and stage a coup d'etat (overthrow). The members of the Directory, therefore, agreed to Napoleon's proposed Egyptian campaign.

Napoleon prepared for the campaign in early 1798. His officers assembled troops, supplies, ships, and weapons along the coasts of southern France, Italy, and Corsica. To keep the purpose of the expedition a secret from English spies, the French government officially labeled the gathering force as the Army of England, thereby suggesting that Britain itself was slated for invasion. Although he had indeed planned an invasion of England, Napoleon believed such an effort was premature. Egypt must come first.

## Napoleon's Army Sets Sail

In hindsight, even the groundwork for Napoleon's rise to power displays one of his great failings. He was a brilliant tactician but an impatient military planner. He rushed the preparations for Egypt and ignored warnings from his staff officers that many of the French ships were in bad repair, that experienced crews to sail them were lacking, and that the powerful British navy would easily defeat them if the two fleets encountered each other.

Under Napoleon's orders, a force of fifty-six warships and more than fifty thousand soldiers and sailors embarked from five different ports on May 19, 1798. In the meantime, an English fleet under the command of Rear Admiral Sir Horatio Nelson scoured the Mediter-

*French warships led by Napoleon bombard and conquer the island of Malta before sailing on to Egypt in 1798.*

ranean, searching for the French convoys. After conquering Malta, an island lying between Sicily and the coast of North Africa, Napoleon continued to Alexandria, Egypt's principal seaport, which fell to the French on July 2.

As the French prepared to march inland to the Egyptian capital of Cairo, however, Napoleon's rushed preparations and his disregard of the advice of his aides began to affect his army. Napoleon had not ordered a reconnaissance of Egypt in advance, nor had he ordered maps of the country to be prepared. As a result, the French did not know the location of important roads, of food depots used by the Mamelukes, or of water wells. Their transport was inadequate, as were the supplies of food and water brought from home. As a result, many soldiers died of hunger and thirst in a scorching desert.

Napoleon pushed the army relentlessly, determined to meet and defeat the army of the Mamelukes. The confrontation finally came on July 21, when the massed French infantry defeated a Mameluke

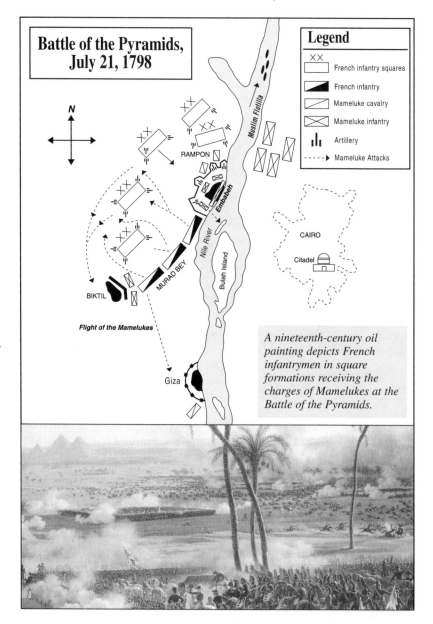

## Battle of the Pyramids, July 21, 1798

### Legend

| | |
|---|---|
| French infantry squares | |
| French infantry | |
| Mameluke cavalry | |
| Mameluke infantry | |
| Artillery | |
| Mameluke Attacks | |

N

RAMPON

Muslim Flotilla

Embabeh

Nile River

Bulah Island

CAIRO

Citadel

BIKTIL

MURAD BEY

Flight of the Mamelukes

Giza

*A nineteenth-century oil painting depicts French infantrymen in square formations receiving the charges of Mamelukes at the Battle of the Pyramids.*

army on the western side of the Nile River, in sight of the famous ancient pyramids of Giza. Victory in this Battle of the Pyramids allowed Napoleon to advance and capture Cairo, the Egyptian capital.

In the meantime, however, Admiral Nelson and the English had located the French fleet at Aboukir Bay, east of Alexandria. It proved an auspicious time for the English to attack. The French sailors suffered many of the same problems as did the soldiers on land. Ignoring the warnings of his officers, Napoleon had thrown all of his resources into the land campaign, leaving the navy to fend for itself. As a result, the army quartermasters often refused to send food or fresh water out to the ships, and sailors were deserting merely to save themselves from starvation. The fleet was undermanned and unprepared for a major battle as a result.

At Aboukir Bay on August 1, Nelson inflicted a total defeat on the French navy. This left Napoleon's land forces isolated, with no means of reinforcing or resupplying themselves. Napoleon showed little concern. Historian Jacques Bainville sums up Napoleon's blithe attitude toward the dangers and hardships faced by his officers and men:

> [I]t is striking to note how little this disaster [the naval defeat at Aboukir Bay] affected Bonaparte. His expedition had no more ships? It would do without them. It could not count on supplies from abroad? It would be organized to live on the occupied country and to produce necessities on the spot. The commander-in-chief was not disturbed for a moment. Difficulties seemed to stimulate him.[4]

Despite the loss of his entire Mediterranean fleet, Napoleon would not admit that he had been beaten. He set up headquarters in Cairo, moving into a magnificent Mameluke palace that he believed fit his status as the most important man in Egypt. He appointed a divan, or nine-member assembly, to govern the new French colony. The French appointed obedient Egyptian ministers to oversee agriculture, industry, roads, and taxes; the French also seized the property and money of the Mameluke rulers.

Not only was he cut off, but the colonization of Egypt turned out to be much more difficult than Napoleon had expected. The Egyptians, Napoleon discovered, were surprisingly reluctant to embrace French rule. In the fall and winter of 1798–1799, Napoleon scattered his army divisions up and down the Nile in an attempt to quell a rebellion among the Egyptians and the nomadic desert dwellers known as the Bedouin, who staged constant hit-and-run raids against French forts, supply trains, and patrols. In one particularly violent incident, Napoleon responded to an uprising in Cairo itself by ordering the public execution of hundreds of prisoners and the destruction of the al-Azhar Mosque, one of the city's holiest Muslim shrines.

Meanwhile, Napoleon was paying little heed to the many ills that were slowly destroying his army. With the English blockading Alexandria, Egypt's main port, supplies of food and ammunition

*The French assault the fortress at Acre. Overcoming the town's fortified stone walls and protective guns proved impossible.*

were running low. The troops suffered from the desert heat and from diseases such as dysentery, which was caused by drinking contaminated water. There was no money coming from France to pay expenses, with the result that French officers were unable to buy needed food or to pay their men. These officers grew increasingly angry with their commander, who seemed to focus on his own personal glory and advancement. Frustrated with Napoleon's grandiose and arrogant attitude, nearly every ranking officer requested a transfer back to France.

## The Defeat at Acre

Several of Napoleon's officers advised a retreat from Egypt. He ignored them, believing that the French could still score a decisive victory that would secure Egypt as a French colony. To achieve this, Napoleon planned another grandiose campaign, this time against the army of the Ottoman Empire. He would march north to the Ottoman province of Syria, capture the Syrian capital of Damascus, and from there threaten Istanbul (formerly Constantinople), the Ottoman capital.

The French army set out from Egypt on January 31, 1799. In mid-March, Napoleon called a halt at the fortified town of Acre, in what is now Israel. Thick stone walls and long rows of powerful guns protected this powerful fortification. After the French began their siege, the Ottoman army counterattacked from the north. On April 16, 1799, Napoleon outmaneuvered and defeated the Turks at the Battle of Mount Tabor. Acre still resisted, and Napoleon ordered a series of bombardments and assaults on the fortress. The attacks failed completely, resulting only in thousands of French casualties. His forces weakening, and short on food and water, Napoleon decided to give up the siege and return to Egypt.

Napoleon put the best face on this setback. In fact, when speaking to his defeated troops, he described the campaign in Syria as a victory. In his order of the day to his Army of the East, written May 17, 1799, he boasted:

Soldiers, you have crossed the desert dividing Africa from Asia faster than an Arab army.

The army that was marching to invade Egypt has been destroyed; you have captured its general, its field equipment,

# The Explosion of the *Orient*

*A British armada attacks French warships with cannon fire at the Battle of Aboukir Bay.*

On the afternoon of August 1, 1799, Admiral Nelson's armada arrived off Aboukir Bay. Determined not to give the French captains time to prepare for battle, Nelson gave the order to attack immediately. The British ships divided into two lines and sailed on either side of the anchored French warships, pouring cannon fire into the enemy's hulls and masts.

The fight lasted the entire night, with both sides suffering heavy casualties. A little after 10 P.M., the French flagship *Orient* exploded in an enormous ball of fire. The detonation of the *Orient* was heard and felt as far away as Alexandria, more than twenty miles to the west. Most of the ship's crew and the commander of the French fleet, Admiral Breuys, were killed instantly. For a short time, British and French sailors and officers were in a state of shock, and guns on both sides fell silent.

The destruction of the *Orient* marked the beginning of the end for the French fleet. With their commander dead and their principal ship destroyed, the French ships began scattering around Aboukir Bay, unable to coordinate their defenses. The explosion boosted the morale of Nelson's sailors and cannon crews, inspiring them to greater efforts against the enemy. In the hours that followed the explosion of the *Orient*, the remaining ships of the French fleet, except for three vessels that made their escape from the bay, were either destroyed or captured.

its waterskins, its camels. You have taken all the forts defending the desert wells.

... In a few days you might have hoped to capture the Pasha [the Ottoman ruler of Acre] himself in his palace; but at this time of year the capture of the castle of Acre is not worth the loss of a few days, and, besides, the brave men I should lose there are now needed for more essential operations.[5]

Napoleon's retreat to Cairo did not end the hostilities with the Ottomans, who attacked and briefly occupied the French fortress at Aboukir Bay. Napoleon recaptured this fortress, but seeing no further opportunity for glory in Egypt, he decided to return to France. Claiming that his presence there was needed to stem attacks by France's European enemies, he slipped away from the port of Alexandria on August 23, leaving behind a French force that by this time numbered about fifteen thousand men—fewer than one-third of the troops that had set out from France.

Napoleon's disastrous campaign had cost the lives of more than forty thousand soldiers and sailors. More ominously, the destruction of the French navy at Aboukir Bay had left the British in complete command of the Mediterranean. In March 1799, the British had captured the French-held island of Corfu, off the western coast of Greece. In September, the British captured the French garrison at Malta. In 1801, British troops would land on the coast of Egypt and seize the road linking Alexandria to Cairo. With their communications and supplies cut off, the remaining French garrison would be forced to surrender.

## Return to France

Fortunately for Napoleon, word of France's reversals in Egypt and elsewhere traveled slowly. After a sea voyage lasting six weeks, Napoleon arrived in the small port of Saint-Raphael on the Mediterranean coast of France on October 9, 1799. Instead of condemning him for abandoning his army, the French people hailed Napoleon as a great conqueror.

Thanks to this popularity, Napoleon found himself well positioned to take control of the French government. On November 9, 1799, with the help of his brother Lucien Bonaparte, Napoleon

*In a chaotic scene at the palace of Saint-Cloud, the French Directory is overthrown in favor of a new Consulate headed by Napoleon.*

overthrew the Directory and dispersed the legislature at gunpoint. On November 12, Napoleon announced that the French constitution, which had gone into effect in 1795, was dead. Under a new constitution, the five-man Directory was replaced with a three-member Consulate. In an election that Napoleon carefully rigged, he was chosen to head this new governing body.

Napoleon had become the new king of France in all but name. He began to see himself as the successor to the great rulers of the past: the ancient Roman leader Caesar and the medieval Frankish emperor Charlemagne. He also saw himself as the only man who could lead

France out of its revolutionary chaos and back to its rightful position as the leading power in Europe. France was on a mission—the liberation of Europe from monarchy—and he would be the one to lead that mission.

Napoleon and many French leaders may not have realized that many Europeans were not interested in republican government. As historian Michael Broers writes:

> Only a few months before [Napoleon's] coup . . . the new regime had a foretaste of how deeply the people of western Europe had come to hate the French, the conduct of their armies, their revolutionary ideas. . . . In 1798, the Belgian departments and almost the whole of Italy had been the theatres of large, widespread counter-revolutionary uprisings. . . . They were the culmination of several years of upheaval, caused in part by the transitory ravages of war—usually in the shape of the French armies.[6]

Napoleon had reached a pinnacle of power within France. Ultimately, however, the defeat in Egypt would have long-term effects on France. English mastery over the Mediterranean would help to overcome a French blockade, known as the Continental System, of English trade. The French navy, weakened by the defeat at Aboukir Bay, would not recover, and in fact would suffer another major loss to the English at the Battle of Trafalgar in 1805.

In the meantime, Napoleon's arrogance—his failure to listen to and consider the opinions and experience of others—would so exasperate his officers and the French people that he would lose all support at home. In the end, Napoleon's unwillingness or inability

 **The Code Napoleon**

As first consul, Napoleon completely remodeled the French government and administration. The nation's finances were reorganized, and the Bank of France was established. A set of federal laws known as the Code Napoleon was written, sweeping away the jumbled, chaotic, and confusing laws of the old monarchy. Napoleon took a personal hand in the writing of the new laws, and the Code Napoleon went into effect in 1804. The Code Napoleon remains the basis of the French legal system, and in later years Napoleon would often refer to it as his single greatest achievement.

to regard others as his equals would prove his undoing. The French writer Germaine de Stael, whom Napoleon would exile from France in 1803, described his personality as follows:

> He regarded a human being as an action or a thing, not as a fellow creature. He did not hate any more than he loved; for him nothing existed but himself. . . . He was an able chess-player, and the human race was the opponent to whom he proposed to give check-mate. His successes depended as much on the qualities which he lacked as on the talents which he possessed. Neither pity, nor religion, not attachment to any idea whatsoever, could [deflect] him from his principal direction.[7]

In Napoleon Bonaparte, arrogance went hand in hand with unlimited ambition. Always in quest of new battlefields on which to win his glory, Napoleon could not rest, could not be satisfied with what he had already achieved. The lives of his soldiers, the reputation of France, the state of the French treasury, and even members of his own family would be sacrificed for the sake of power. For Napoleon, there was nothing to consider outside of his standing in the world and his personal success, and there would be no end to his quest to achieve that success.

# Failed Economics: The Continental System

**Chapter 2**

N APOLEON VIEWED THE world through the eyes of a military strategist, seeing the nations around him as rivals to be defeated or humbled. There could be no peaceful coexistence with these countries on a basis of equality, and especially not with England, France's principal military and political rival for more than five centuries. From a military standpoint, England presented Napoleon with a problem. The British navy remained the master of the seas, making an invasion by France impossible. To achieve what he considered his most important victory, Napoleon adopted a different strategy: economic warfare.

Napoleon knew that the English relied on their overseas colonies to provide such staples as sugar, coffee, indigo, cotton, rum, and tobacco. English traders sold these goods on the European continent or used them to make manufactured goods, which could in turn be sold on the Continent or to their own colonies, which had little manufacturing capacity of their own. Napoleon believed that a blockade that prevented these raw materials from reaching England or finished goods from being exported would weaken England's economy, forcing the English to acknowledge French mastery of the Continent.

This blockade, known as the Continental System to historians, would prove to be a major miscalculation on Napoleon's part. What he failed to understand was that, for many reasons, a continent-wide ban on English trade could not be enforced, even in France itself. As historian Michael Glover writes:

> The fact was that it was impossible to stop British goods reaching Europe. London encouraged smuggling on the largest scale.

# Remaking Paris in the Image of Rome

*Napoleon commissioned architects to decorate Paris with great monuments reminiscent of Rome, like the massive Arc de Triomphe (above) and Colonne Vendôme (below).*

Napoleon saw himself in the mold of the ancient Roman emperors, who left behind great monuments to glorify their accomplishments. He remade the French capital of Paris, ordering the nation's leading architects to design great columns, arches, and triumphant monuments to make the city into an imperial capital.

New bridges were raised across the Seine, the river that bisects Paris. New boulevards cut through the capital's tangled medieval quarters as entire neighborhoods were razed to the ground. Napoleon's architects designed the Quai d'Orsay (foreign ministry) and the Bourse (stock market) to resemble the ancient temples of Greece and Rome. The Arc de Triomphe, standing at the western end of a wide avenue known as the Champs-Elysees (Elysian Fields), glorified Napoleon's military victories and his generals. Most of these monumental structures and avenues have survived in modern Paris, a city that in many ways reflects Napoleon's unbounded ambition and sense of grandeur.

At one end of Europe Heligoland [on the North Sea coast] was seized from the Danes and used as a centre for small boats plying to and from the north German ports. At the other, sugar was landed at [the Greek port of] Salonika (then Turkish), packed in . . . boxes and taken on muleback over the Balkans and through Serbia before being sold in central Europe, much of it going on to France.[8]

## Preparing for the Continental System

As Napoleon set out to seal off as much of Europe as he could from trade with England, France's army swept into northern Italy, which was then ruled by Austria, in the spring of 1800. Napoleon easily outmaneuvered the Austrian armies, decisively defeating them on June 14 at the Battle of Marengo. The French under General Jean Moreau defeated the Austrians again at the Battle of Hohenlinden in December 1800. After this second defeat, the Austrians signed the Peace of Luneville on February 9, 1801, ceding northern Italy, land west of the Rhine River, and all of Belgium to France.

This victory was not enough to secure the Continent, however. The British remained masters of the Mediterranean, thanks in part to Napoleon's bungled Egyptian campaign. To keep English goods from entering Europe through Spain, at the western limit of the Mediterranean, Napoleon signed the Treaty of Aranjuez on March 21, 1801, under which France allied itself with Spain and placed the Spanish market off-limits to English goods. By another treaty signed on June 6, 1801, England's longtime ally and trading partner Portugal agreed to stop trading with England.

## First Consul for Life

At first, the Continental System seemed to work. Knowing its people were growing weary of the sacrifices demanded by war, the English government decided to negotiate with Napoleon. By the Treaty of Amiens, signed on March 25, 1802, by France, Holland, Spain, and England, Egypt was returned to the Ottoman Turks; the English-occupied Cape of Good Hope, at the southern tip of Africa, was returned to the Dutch. England agreed to evacuate Mediterranean ports and return several Caribbean colonies that it had previously seized to

*French and British diplomats sign the Treaty of Amiens in 1802,
redistributing conquered territories and supposedly ending hostilities
between France, England, and Spain.*

France, while the French agreed to pull their forces from Rome—the
seat of the Papal States—and Naples.

The treaty made Napoleon—and his economic challenge to the
English—wildly popular within France. In the next year, the government held a plebiscite, or vote, to extend the term of First Consul
Napoleon for life. The republican principles Napoleon had originally
claimed to believe in would be discarded, and he would become the

nation's monarch. On August 2, 1803, the government announced that Napoleon had won the vote by a total of 3.6 million votes to 8,374. In fact, the plebiscite was a total fraud, as Lucien Bonaparte, Napoleon's brother, who was placed in control of counting the votes, simply discarded the vast majority of ballots that had gone against his brother.

Being elected as first consul for life inspired Napoleon with a new ambition: to establish a hereditary monarchy in France. There was no one in France or in the rest of Europe able to challenge him, and so this time there was no plebiscite. Napoleon simply ordered his own coronation, an event that took place on December 2, 1804, at the cathedral of Notre Dame in Paris, and which formally established what historians call the First Empire.

## The Berlin Decree

Despite his new title, Napoleon still had not yet mastered the entire European continent, nor was France able to control every European port. There were not enough ships to patrol the harbors and not enough troops to supervise the docks and customhouses. As a result, the blockade proved ineffective in the ports where it was legally in force. Furthermore, Austria, Prussia, and Russia still dominated central and eastern Europe. Napoleon declared war and led his armies eastward in 1805, smashing the Austrians and Russians at the Battle of Austerlitz, which took place north of the Austrian capital of Vienna.

The Battle of Austerlitz, one of the most important of Napoleon's career, humiliated the Austrian emperor Francis I as well as the Russian czar (emperor) Alexander I, yet it did not seal the blockade of Europe as Napoleon had hoped. In the next year, the English used their navy to counter Napoleon's threat to close Scandinavian ports and stop trade through the Baltic Sea. The English sailed to Copenhagen, the capital of Denmark, and demanded the total surrender of the Danish fleet. When the Danes, in fear of French retaliation, refused to surrender their fleet, the English bombarded Copenhagen on September 2, 1806. The city quickly fell, and the English seized eight Danish ships to prevent Napoleon from seizing them himself.

In the meantime, Napoleon carried on negotiations with Russia, a vast and distant empire that remained well beyond the reach of the

Continental System. After Austerlitz, Napoleon believed he had only to lay down terms for the Russian czar to accept. But faced with heavy territorial and economic demands from Napoleon, Alexander refused to come to terms. Napoleon immediately called up more troops and prepared for a campaign in the fall of 1806. Once again, France prevailed, gaining victories against Russia and Russia's military ally, Prussia, at the Battles of Jena and Auerstadt on October 14, 1806.

With Prussia, Austria, and Russia now reeling from their military defeats, Napoleon felt ready to tighten the economic noose around the English. Following a victory procession into Berlin, the Prussian capital, in November 1806, he issued the Berlin Decree, which set up a total French blockade against England: No ship arriving from English ports or colonies could dock in any French-controlled port.

The decree read, in part:

All commerce and correspondence with the British isles are forbidden. . . .

Every individual who is an English subject, of whatever state or condition he may be, who shall be discovered in any country occupied by our troops or by those of our allies, shall be made a prisoner of war. . . .

All warehouses, merchandise or property of whatever kind belonging to a subject of England shall be regarded as a lawful prize. . . .

No vessel coming directly from England or from the English colonies or which shall have visited these since the publication of the present decree shall be received in any port.

Any vessel contravening the above provision by a false declaration shall be seized, and the vessel and cargo shall be confiscated as if it were English property.[9]

Yet the blockade still had holes in it that prevented it from effectively shutting down the English economy. For one thing, the English were in complete control of the seas. At the Battle of Trafalgar in 1805, the English had smashed the French and Spanish navies, the remnants of which took shelter in the Spanish port of Cadiz. As a result, ships carrying English trade goods were free to call at any port

## The Bonaparte Dynasties

*Louis Bonaparte was appointed king of Holland in 1806 by Napoleon, but was forced to abdicate.*

After Napoleon's sweeping victory at the Battle of Austerlitz, it seemed that no state in Europe would ever have the military power to oppose French dominance of the Continent. Napoleon saw this as an opportunity to extend the French domain by using the members of his own family as puppet rulers of the territories he had conquered.

He appointed his brother Louis as the king of Holland in March 1806. But Louis stymied his brother's ambition in many ways, most importantly by defying the Continental System in the interest of keeping Holland peaceful and prosperous. Napoleon also named Joseph as the king of Naples, a domain covering the southern part of the Italian peninsula and Sicily. Later Napoleon demanded that Joseph serve as the puppet king of Spain—an assignment that Joseph reluctantly accepted and halfheartedly carried out. Jerome Bonaparte became the king of Westphalia, the principal state of the Napoleonic creation known as the Confederation of the Rhine. Jerome's mismanagement and corruption soon made him many enemies among his subjects and his ministers, and he was easily driven out of his kingdom by the Allied advance across northern Germany in 1813.

Napoleon's manipulation of his siblings did not always meet with agreement. When he demanded that his brother Lucien divorce his wife, Alexandrine, who was a commoner, Lucien refused. Instead of bowing to the pressure Lucien fled Italy for England—an act that Napoleon saw as a terrible betrayal.

*Napoleon's eldest brother, Joseph Bonaparte, was named king of Naples and, later, puppet king of Spain.*

*A British armada under Admiral Horatio Nelson attacks French and Spanish fleets at Cape Trafalgar. Nelson's decisive victory ended Napoleon's naval power.*

not directly controlled by France. For example, English trade with Portugal continued, providing a vital trading route to Spain as well. With no fear of interference at sea, the English could also freely trade with their colonies in the Caribbean.

Even where Napoleon's control should have been unquestioned, as in kingdoms where Napoleon had placed his own brothers on the throne, trade continued. Smuggling through ports on the North Sea became a big business, as described by J. Christopher Herold in *The Age of Napoleon:*

> Smuggling was practiced on a heroic scale and became the most lucrative form of business in Europe. Smugglers plied their trade back and forth across the [English] Channel almost every night and on foggy days. From the coast of

northwest Germany long wagon trains of contraband goods clogged the roads into the interior, with connivance of Napoleon's own brother, King Jerome of Westphalia.[10]

Other brothers of Napoleon were defying the Continental System as well, since they knew that complying with the blockade would hurt their own subjects and eventually threaten their own power. For example, the English traded freely with Holland, where Napoleon's brother Louis Bonaparte, whom the emperor had appointed king, turned a blind eye. The kingdom of Naples, under the rule of Joseph Bonaparte, kept its ports open as well.

Even Napoleon's countrymen worked against the Continental System. French officials made fortunes by smuggling or by issuing

 ## The Confederation of the Rhine

Throughout his reign, Napoleon greatly feared an invasion of his country from the east. To avoid this, he created a buffer state lying east of the Rhine. By the Act of Confederation, signed on July 12, 1806, the Confederation of the Rhine was established. More than 350 small principalities, electorates, and free cities of Germany were reorgnized into thirty-nine states. These states would send annual subsidies to the French treasury and would be obliged to pay for maintaining the French troops garrisoned within their frontiers. Each of the states also sent representatives to a Diet (representative assembly) in Frankfurt. The chief of state of the Confederation was Elector-Archbishop duc de Dalberg, a close ally of Napoleon who was determined to carry forward French interests east of the Rhine. The kingdom of Westphalia, ruled by Napoleon's brother Jerome, was the largest state within the confederation—but misrule and corruption on the part of Jerome made Westphalia a very reluctant ally of France.

The Confederation of the Rhine was strongly opposed by Austria, which sought to keep the German states disunited and weak. The king of Prussia remained neutral toward Napoleon until the confederation began posing a military threat, a threat made worse by the annexation of Prussia's traditional rival, Saxony, into the Napoleonic state. This action roused the Prussian king out of his neutrality. Prussian armies were recruited and trained, and, in 1812 and after Napoleon's total defeat in Russia, the Prussian king began signing treaties with the Allied coalition that also included England, Austria, and Russia. In 1813, as the Allies swept west after the defeat of Napoleon at the Battle of Leipzig, the Confederation of the Rhine disintegrated, and the buffer state Napoleon had created disappeared from the map of Europe.

private permits for English merchants to trade within their territories.
It proved impossible for Napoleon's administration to completely enforce the embargo.

## The Treaty of Tilsit

Despite the evidence that his economic warfare was ineffective even
in territory he controlled, Napoleon looked to extend the Continental
System by defeating Russia. With this objective in mind, he led another military campaign through the winter of 1806–1807 and finally
achieved a victory against the Russians at the Battle of Friedland on
June 14, 1807. After this humiliation of his army, Czar Alexander
asked for an armistice. At this point Napoleon had both Russia and
her ally, Prussia, helpless before him. Under terms of the treaty
signed at the Prussian town of Tilsit on July 7, 1807, Prussia would
surrender a large territory to a newly created conglomeration of German states known as the Confederation of the Rhine, whose government was allied with France. The treaty also created the Grand
Duchy of Warsaw, which would be ruled by the king of Saxony,
whose realm was part of the Confederation of the Rhine. Russia
agreed to recognize the French allies of Holland, Naples, and Westphalia, as well as the entire Confederation of the Rhine. The ports of
Stockholm and Copenhagen, as well as the Kattegat Strait lying between Denmark and Sweden, were closed to the English, cutting
them off from trade with Russia through the Baltic Sea.

Before the treaty was signed, Napoleon and Alexander had met
on a raft in the middle of the Nieman River, the dividing line between
the armies of Russia and France. The two rulers talked for long
hours, professing great friendship and admiration for each other, and
promising an end to their rivalry in Europe. But both men knew that
the Treaty of Tilsit, rather than a friendly agreement, represented a
direct challenge to Russian power. Napoleon was contesting control
of Poland, which the Russian czars had ruled, or indirectly controlled,
for centuries.

The Treaty of Tilsit made Napoleon overconfident and reckless.
He was now certain that he had finally mastered Europe and had
ended any threat to France from Russia. Historian Jacques Bainville
explains: "Napoleon felt that only a few years of alliance with the
greatest power on the Continent [Russia] would suffice to make him

*Russian czar Alexander (right) and Napoleon discuss the extensive terms of the Treaty of Tilsit.*

irresistible. The underlying principle of his gravest errors lay there. He was a victim of the Russian mirage. He was not the first, and would not be the last."[11]

After signing the treaty, Napoleon extended the Continental System to affect any nation that dared to defy the blockade. By the Milan Decree of December 1807, France claimed the right to confiscate any ships and goods that had been in English ports, no matter what nation owned these ships and goods. The decree also stated that any ship paying taxes or duties of any kind to England would be subject to seizure by France. Even a ship that allowed itself to be searched by the English risked capture.

The blockade did have some effect in England. The people suffered shortages of vital goods they had ordinarily imported. Bankruptcies increased, exports fell sharply, prices rose, and unemployment increased as mills and factories shut down for lack of raw materials. But the English fought back by issuing their own decree, declaring a blockade of France and its allies in Europe. French companies found themselves without markets for their goods. Hundreds of businesses and banks failed. Staple goods imported from British colonies became expensive, often impossible to find in French markets: coffee, sugar, tea, and cotton. Unemployment, poverty, and discontent rose within France, while the governments of France and of several other allied nations nearly went bankrupt. Ultimately these hardships would turn the French and the rest of an impoverished Europe against Napoleon.

## The Pope and the Continental System

Napoleon still believed that he only needed to make the Continental System tougher by plugging the leaks and backing up the blockade with military force and political maneuvering. He knew that Italy, with its long coastlines and fragmented political landscape, represented a key weakness in the Continental System. British ships and smugglers still brought their goods into the Italian ports of Civitavecchia, Rimini, and Ancona. The Papal States, small principalities of central Italy that were directly ruled by the Roman Catholic Church, remained open to English goods and merchants. In addition, the pope, who as the spiritual leader of the Catholic Church was one of the most influential figures in Italy, refused to cooperate with Napoleon. In his actions and his words as first consul and then as emperor, Napoleon showed little respect for the pope or the Church. As a result, the pope stayed neutral whenever France went to war, in spite of the fact that the great majority of French people were devout Catholics.

Napoleon knew that the people of France felt a strong loyalty to the Church and the pope. Yet, although he saw the church as a rival for the support of the French populace, he was supremely confident that he was more than a match for the pope. In July 1807, he was heard to say: "perhaps the time is not far off when I will recognize the Pope only as the Bishop of Rome, equal in rank to any of the other bishops of my realms. I am not afraid . . . to conduct my business without the pope."[12]

It was not long before Napoleon chose to test the pope's power directly. On April 1, 1808, Napoleon demanded that the pope arrest British diplomats in Rome and close all ports within the Papal States to the British. On the next day, before the pope could even respond, French troops entered Rome and enforced Napoleon's demands. The French eventually seized the remaining ports in the Italian peninsula.

*Under Napoleon's order, Pope Pius VII is arrested in Rome for failing to comply with the French emperor's Continental System.*

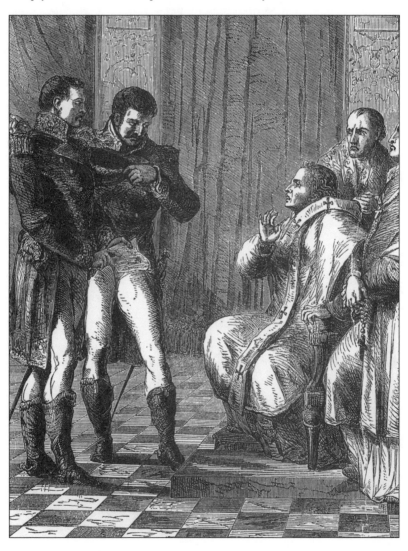

These strong-arm tactics brought a strong reaction—the most drastic measure the pope could take against any secular ruler. On June 1, 1809, the pope excommunicated Napoleon, effectively cutting him off from the Church, since this move banned him from all holy places (including churches) and denied him the sacraments necessary for salvation. In the next month, Napoleon retaliated by ordering that the pope be taken prisoner. The pope would be held captive at Napoleon's palace of Fontainebleau, near Paris, until January 1814.

The Continental System now included Italy, but still there were gaps in the blockade. Portugal had been ignoring Napoleon and the Continental System and keeping all of its ports open to the British. Napoleon reacted with a fatal overconfidence, believing that his *Grande Armée* was invincible and that no nation could stand up to it. He ordered an invasion of Portugal, intending to enforce the Continental System at one of England's vital trading points. If the occupation of Portugal proved successful, he planned to use Portugal as a jumping-off point for a conquest of the entire Iberian Peninsula. When the French general Andoche Junot led the Army of Observation of the Pyrenees across Spain and into Lisbon, the capital of Portugal, in the autumn of 1807, the Peninsular War was under way—and the unraveling of Napoleon's empire began.

# The Peninsular War:The Emperor Overreaches

**Chapter 3**

THE TREATY OF TILSIT brought Napoleon and the French Empire to the height of their power in Europe. Napoleon had now humbled the Continent's three greatest military powers: Austria, Prussia, and Russia. His brother Jerome served him as the king of Westphalia, part of the Confederation of the Rhine. Joseph Bonaparte ruled in the kingdom of Naples, in southern Italy. Louis Bonaparte reigned in Holland. Within France, Napoleon's popularity was high, his authority unquestioned.

Yet Napoleon realized that military success—not personal popularity—had made him master of the rest of Europe. As Napoleon himself wrote: "My power depends on my glory and my glories on the victories I have won. My power will fall if I do not feed it on new glories and new victories. Conquest has made me what I am and only conquest can enable me to hold my position."[13]

## A Latter-Day Charlemagne

A diligent student of history, Napoleon saw himself as a latter-day Charlemagne, the emperor of the Franks whose power stretched across western Europe in the early ninth century. Napoleon intended to establish a dynasty modeled on that of Charlemagne's Carolingian, with the Bonaparte brothers and his own heirs serving as his useful and obedient puppets.

Napoleon did not realize that to be a Charlemagne in early nineteenth-century Europe was a different task altogether. He had committed France and its allied governments to the defense of a huge realm—a state simply too big for one man, or even one family, to

control. Eventually, this overreaching would contribute to his downfall. Historian James Marshall-Cornwall writes:

> The French Empire now extended from the Pyrenees to the
> Elbe, a distance of 900 miles as the crow files; in the south it
> continued to the toe of Italy, and in the east to the Dalmatian
> coast. The problems of administering such a vast area, peo-
> pled by so many different nations, were becoming too great
> a burden to be carried by one ruler, especially one who had
> such a meticulous mind for detail.[14]

One of Napoleon's ablest ministers, Charles-Maurice de Talleyrand, often pointed out this problem and advised Napoleon to rein in
his ambition and bring France and the rest of Europe a period of peace.
But Napoleon did not tolerate what he considered criticism from his
ministers. Believing the French army to be invincible, he saw no reason
to listen to contrary voices. Taking Talleyrand's advice as a personal in-
sult, Napoleon had excluded him from the Tilsit negotiations and had
gladly accepted Talleyrand's resignation in July 1807. The obliging

*Charles-Maurice de
Talleyrand, a minister
to Napoleon who
urged the emperor to
strive for peace in
Europe, resigned in
1807.*

Nompere de Champagny, who would not stand up to Napoleon or criticize his decisions, took Talleyrand's position as foreign minister.

## The Campaign in Iberia

Napoleon dreamed of extending France's sway all the way to the Ottoman Empire, Mesopotamia, and India—following in the path of the ancient Macedonian king Alexander the Great. This ambition dovetailed with Napoleon's practical need to tighten his blockade of England's foreign trade. In order to tighten the blockade, Napoleon decided the time had come to gain complete control over the Iberian Peninsula—in other words, Spain and Portugal. In the process, Napoleon also hoped to conquer the English naval base at Gibraltar, in southern Spain at the junction of the Mediterranean Sea and the Atlantic Ocean. Accomplishing this, Napoleon believed, would drive the English from the Continent altogether and close off the Mediterranean to English shipping.

To conquer Spain, Napoleon intended to overthrow Spain's Bourbon dynasty—cousins to the Bourbons who had ruled France before the Revolution—and place one of his brothers on the Spanish throne. Napoleon's task was made easier by the fact that the Spanish royal family was divided and easily manipulated. The king's government was further weakened by the ambitious intrigues of Manuel de Godoy, a royal adviser who by his scheming had made himself the most powerful individual in the kingdom.

Napoleon's plan began with the secret Treaty of Fontainebleau, signed on October 27, 1807. In return for being allowed to use Spain as a staging area for an invasion of Portugal, Napoleon promised to divide Portugal with Spain. Godoy would be given his own private realm in southern Portugal, in exchange for going along with Napoleon's demand that all ports be closed to the British. The treaty offered Spain's king Charles IV the opportunity to settle a long-standing rivalry with Portugal on favorable terms. Charles may also have believed he could control Napoleon's ambitions in Iberia. If so, that was a mistake.

Napoleon ordered his army to cross Spanish territory and invade Portugal in November. But, as in the Egyptian campaign, he paid little attention to essential reconnaissance and preparation, so problems soon arose. The French army was poorly supplied, and the English

*Spanish king Charles IV (pictured) and his son Ferdinand were duped into giving Napoleon legal claim to the throne of Spain.*

navy threatened its lines of communication and supply by sea (supply across the high Pyrenees mountain range proved difficult, especially during winter). By the time the French had reached Portugal's capital, Lisbon, thousands of soldiers were dying of hunger and disease.

Disregarding the difficulties, Napoleon quickly turned on his Spanish ally, ordering his armies to occupy Spanish cities. On February 16, 1808, the French moved on Spain's principal northern cities of Pamplona, Barcelona, and San Sebastian. Meanwhile, Napoleon's strategy of exploiting rivalries within the royal family began to succeed. Ferdinand, the son of King Charles IV, made an appeal to Napoleon to assist him in claiming the Spanish throne from his father.

When the French continued southward, the Bourbons fled toward the port of Cadiz. The king was stopped before reaching Cadiz and abdicated in favor of his son—then changed his mind. Napoleon then summoned the entire royal family and Godoy to the southern French port of Bayonne. He also ordered General Joachim Murat to seize Spain's capital of Madrid, which was accomplished on March 24.

## Outfoxing the Bourbons of Spain

The Bourbons had obeyed Napoleon's summons to Bayonne, arriving at the French port on April 30. In two secret meetings, Napoleon outmaneuvered the Spanish royal family, first convincing Charles to temporarily give up his throne in favor of Napoleon, then convincing Ferdinand to surrender his claim to the throne in favor of his father. By these agreements, Charles and Ferdinand had both surrendered any legal claim to the Spanish throne.

Meanwhile, the emperor searched among his brothers for someone to ascend the throne of Spain and serve as his obedient puppet, but his siblings were reluctant to accept. First Lucien, then Louis, then Jerome all declined the offer. Finally Joseph, whom Napoleon had already installed as the king of Naples, reluctantly accepted the

## A Spat with Josephine

By the time of the Peninsular War, Napoleon's endless quest for military conquest and glory was beginning to wear down the loyalty of his officers, his ministers, and even his wife. More significantly, Napoleon was beginning to feel himself losing control and to see himself as trapped in an exhausting round of marches and maneuvers. In his book *Napoleon*, historian Jacques Bainville describes the argument brought about by the emperor's exhausting Iberian adventure and a telling retort made by the emperor to the empress Josephine:

> Napoleon set off reluctantly and listlessly for the Pyrenees [and Spain] on the 29th [of October, 1808]. Spain wearied him. To fight against peasant bands in this country of fanatics, with enemy ambushes behind every rock, where there was neither government nor state, and consequently no possibility of ending matters with a few thunderbolt marches, was a wearisome toil. "Will you never stop making war?" Josephine asked him. And he retorted in ill humor: "Do you think I enjoy it? You know I can do other things than waging war, but I am the bondslave of necessity; I don't control events, I obey them."

throne of Spain on April 18, 1808. On May 6, the day when Ferdinand gave up his claim, Joseph was proclaimed as the new king. Joseph had to give up Naples, which Napoleon turned over to his brother-in-law, General Murat.

Napoleon believed that occupying and controlling Spain through Joseph Bonaparte would be a simple matter. He believed that well-trained and well-led French troops could overcome any resistance the Spanish might mount. He also believed that the Spanish would welcome a new regime and that they would favor French rule and the ideals of the French Revolution over the despotic Bourbon dynasty. The logistical problems of supplying an occupation force in Spain did not interest him. Nor was he worried about the problems of providing reinforcements, or the fact that France still needed large garrisons to keep the peace in the other European nations that already had come under French control.

## Spain Revolts

Napoleon also had not considered the growing spirit of nationalism, which the French Revolution had inspired throughout Europe. The

people of Spain, like the people of Germany and Italy, were beginning to see themselves as a single nation, in which a common lan-
guage, culture, and history tied together distant regions and cities.
Nor did Napoleon count on the resistance of the people of Spain to
rule by a foreigner—a Bonaparte. As historian Rafael Altamira
writes:

> Like the rest of Europe, [Napoleon] had believed that the
> only opposition to him in Spain would come from the
> courtiers and the army. Through his own dealings with
> Godoy and [Spanish king] Ferdinand VII, he had learned to
> despise the former. With regard to the army, he knew his

*French soldiers surrender to an army of civilians, Spanish rebels, and
Englishmen at Bailen, in southern Spain.*

ground and felt no anxiety. But to his astonishment, he found himself confronted by a nation in arms. Nothing in his experience had taught him how to measure such a force as that.[15]

The first sign of trouble came on May 2, when a revolt broke out in Madrid against the French occupation troops. In the same month, Spanish forces bombarded and captured the French fleet anchored at the port of Cadiz. The rebellion spread as French garrisons occupying important Spanish cities came under attack and entire regions began openly defying their French governors. The Spanish army supported the rebellion against the French, while the leaders of Spain's Catholic Church denounced the French as occupiers and as heretics, rallying the population to the cry of *Dos de Mayo* (the second of May). The Spanish rebel leaders allied themselves with the English, who in turn provided the rebels with arms and money to continue the insurrection. On July 22 came an outright defeat of the French in Andalusia, a region of southern Spain. After looting the city of Cordoba, twenty-five thousand French troops under General Pierre-Antoine Dupont were met and routed at Bailen.

After Dupont's surrender at Bailen, King Joseph Bonaparte, fearing the French garrison at Madrid would be unable to protect him, fled the capital for Burgos, in northern Spain. Meanwhile, the Spanish fortified and further organized themselves, harassing the French supply lines and cutting off all communication between Madrid and France.

## The Loss of Portugal

Napoleon remained in France, believing he could successfully direct this campaign from Paris, but the situation on the Iberian Peninsula continued to deteriorate. The weakened French army missed his inspiring presence and his brilliant battlefield tactics. The English took advantage of the situation and landed at Mondego Bay, on Portugal's Atlantic coast, in August 1808. Under General Arthur Wellesley, the English marched inland and defeated the French at the Battle of Vimeiro on August 21. General Junot surrendered his army and allowed himself to be taken prisoner. The French had lost control of Portugal, after Napoleon's army had suffered its first major defeat on the European continent. The French appearance of invincibility was smashed forever.

After the defeat in Portugal, Joseph Bonaparte came to believe that the French occupation of Spain was doomed. He demanded that he be allowed to return to his kingdom of Naples. He had no stomach for ruling over an occupied and rebellious country. Refusing to abandon his plan for dominating the Iberian Peninsula, Napoleon did not even respond to his brother's demand. He poured more troops and money into Spain, determined to subdue it at any cost. To keep Spain under French control, Napoleon moved French troops from Germany, Italy, and eastern Europe into Spain as reinforcements. This maneuver did little to pacify Spain; moreover, it weakened France's military position in central Europe.

Seeing that his forces were spread too thin, Napoleon called up 140,000 more draftees at home. He also raised an army of Poles and Germans to fight in Spain, and ordered more garrisons within France to send their troops as well. All in all, he ordered more than 300,000 troops into Spain; he also decided to take personal command of the situation. He arrived in early November 1808, determined to make good his boast, made just before leaving Paris:

> I leave in a few days to put myself at the head of my army and, with the help of God, I will crown the King of Spain in Madrid and plant my eagles [military standards] on the ramparts of Lisbon. . . . It is the special blessing that Providence, which has always watched over our armies, should have so

 **Inspiring a New Kind of Painter**

From the violent and terrible period of the Spanish uprising against Napoleon came one of the most celebrated series of artworks, a series of etchings by the Spanish artist Francisco de Goya. Considered by many to be the father of modern art, Goya brought intense, sometimes grotesque realism to his works. One of his most celebrated paintings, known as the *Third of May*, depicts the death of Spanish rebels at the hands of a firing squad. This work, and a series of drawings known as the *Disasters of War*, showed war not as a glorious enterprise but as a grim and pointless scene of cruelty and sadism. Through Francisco de Goya, the Peninsular War changed the methods and vision of European artists and turned them to consider contemporary social reality as a worthy subject of their works.

blinded the English that they have left the protection of the sea and, at last, exposed their troops on the continent.[16]

Napoleon ordered a new offensive to regain Portugal and the areas of Spain controlled by the rebels. But he was blinded by his past successes on the battlefield and failed to take into account the many problems the French army faced in Spain. The cities of Spain were far apart, and the arid countryside provided little in the way of food for the troops or fodder for the horses. The distances to cover and the poor communications made it nearly impossible for the French generals to coordinate their actions. Harried constantly by guerrilla attacks, the French units remained on the defensive, even after Napoleon arrived to take command. Rebels and Spanish civilians targeted French officers and governors for assassination or capture, and they subjected their prisoners to gruesome tortures that served as terrifying examples to the occupiers. In the meantime, the British army advanced from its base in Portugal to march into northern Spain.

All in all, the Iberian campaign would cost Napoleon several hundred thousand troops, whose blood and effort would be wasted in a total defeat. The disaster was due in part to Napoleon's reckless overconfidence in his ability to govern such an enormous empire. In the opinion of some historians, such as Owen Connelly, the Iberian campaign underlies the fall of Napoleon's empire:

> Only in Spain did developments contribute markedly to Napoleon's downfall. "C'est ce qui m'a perdu ["That's what ruined me"]," he said at Saint Helena. Clearly the immense cost of the Spanish venture in lives, money, and material had greatly weakened the empire. . . .
>
> The Spanish war debilitated the empire as did nothing else, and Joseph, in command of French forces at critical times, bears heavy responsibility for its continuance and the eventual loss of Spain. . . . Joseph's good intentions, liberalism, personal magnetism, and—yes—goodness are not in question. He loved his people, forgave their rebellion, betrayals, and insults, wept for them, and labored for their welfare. But he lost the war. He was not of the stuff of warrior-kings; he was not a Napoleon. Can we blame him for that? No. We do not. We simply say he lost Spain.[17]

*Napoleon (on right) and Czar Alexander meet at the German town of Erfurt. The two will agree that France and Russia will combine forces pending wars with England or Austria.*

With the French military being sapped by the war in Spain, Napoleon realized that his defenses were growing weaker in central Europe. He needed to repair his relations with Russia, and to achieve this, Napoleon again met with Czar Alexander, this time at the German town of Erfurt. Historian Jacques Bainville describes Napoleon's goal:

> The idea behind the meeting of crowned heads at Erfurt, in
> the last days of September, was to make plain to Europe the
> unalterable friendship of the two Emperors, to declare it with

compelling brilliancy . . . But the spirit of Erfurt was not what that of Tilsit had been. Alexander had recovered himself. . . . He confided in his sister Catherine: "Bonaparte takes me for a fool. He laughs best who laughs last."[18]

By the Erfurt Convention, signed on October 12, 1808, Russia agreed to ally with France in the event of war with Austria and to join the Continental System against England. Napoleon assumed that once again he had played the sly diplomat, but he was mistaken. Alexander began preparing for war—against his new French ally.

## The Air of Invincibility Ends

The Erfurt Convention shored up Napoleon's eastern flank—at least temporarily—but the difficulties in Spain continued. For a time Napoleon managed to hold off and even push back English forces in Iberia, but the *Grande Armée* suffered from large-scale desertions. Hearing tales of hunger and the terrors of guerrilla warfare, many French recruits deserted even before reaching Spain. As in Egypt, the campaign set French generals against each other; in some cases they refused to obey direct orders or to cooperate with each other.

In France itself, the shortages imposed by the Continental System were ruining the economy, while resentment grew at the conscriptions needed for the Iberian campaign. Historian Michael Glover sums up the failed campaign as follows:

> The decline of Napoleon's empire can best be dated from the moment when Britain decided to reinforce her small force in Portugal, using the manpower of Portugal and Spain to make up for the numbers which she herself could never deploy in the field. Henceforward the French were to be committed to a struggle which cost her armies an average of 50,000 lives a year and which she could never win.[19]

The Iberian campaign had upset the tenuous hold Napoleon's military success and personal charisma had afforded him over the rest of Europe. The war also damaged Napoleon's popularity and credibility with the French people. The French general Thiebault later testified:

> Our shameful disasters in Andalusia, and our evacuation of Portugal had altered our military and political position, and

**Napoleon and the Spanish Constitution**

From the Peninsular War and Napoleon's attempt to impose a new monarchy on Spain came the origins of that nation's modern constitution. Ironically, the career of Joseph Bonaparte played a vital role in the founding of modern Spanish democracy. On July 8, 1808, in their efforts to overcome the French occupation and the reign of Joseph Bonaparte, Spanish political leaders assembled at a parliament known as the Cortes on September 24, 1810. Two years later, on March 12, 1812, the Spanish promulgated their first constitution, known as the Constitution of Cadiz. This document limited royal power, ended feudal privileges, reformed the tax system, and became a model for new constitutions throughout Latin America in the nineteenth century.

Ironically, it would be a Spanish Bourbon ruler who would put a temporary end to the "liberal" state built by the 1812 constitution. In 1814, after the French were driven from Spain, Ferdinand VII became the king of Spain. Having little interest in representative government, Ferdinand revoked the constitution of 1812 and imposed an absolute monarchy on the people who had just thrown off the rule of the Bonapartes.

the prestige of our former invincibility was now effectively destroyed once and for all. . . . The hatred we now faced—this terrible product resulting from the numerous defeats we had inflicted upon our enemies—now awakened the great desire by the whole of Europe to seek revenge against us.[20]

At the same time, although France had soundly defeated the armies of Austria and Prussia, these powerful states still threatened French control of central Europe. Austria could draw on an empire of millions to quickly raise new armies and strike at French forces in central Europe, which had been weakened by the redeployment of troops to Iberia. Prussia could easily make an alliance with Russia and threaten the Grand Duchy of Warsaw, to the east, and the Confederation of the Rhine, to the west. The Napoleonic empire was stretched too thin, and Napoleon's personal authority—based on fear, rather than admiration—began to dissolve.

Despite the Erfurt Convention the czar of Russia was not cooperating with Napoleon. When the French suffered military setbacks against the Austrians during the summer of 1809, Napoleon sent urgent messages to the czar to attack Austria, in accordance with the terms of the Erfurt Convention. But Alexander did nothing, realizing that a defeat of Austria would leave Napoleon free to attack Russia.

Marshall-Cornwall and many other historians see in the Peninsular War the seeds of Napoleon's ultimate military defeat:

> Napoleon's insanely ambitious decision to extend his sway over all Spain and Portugal was the beginning of his downfall. Largely owing to the ineptitude of his enemies, his victories in central Europe had been too easy. He was now hypnotized by his own success and believed himself to be infallible, both in strategy and statecraft. He had proved himself to be the greatest soldier in Europe, and the *Grande Armée* to be invincible; he had outwitted the most astute diplomats and forced all the crowned heads of ancient monarchies to bend the knee to him. It had all gone to his head.[21]

The failure in Iberia did not shake Napoleon's own confidence, however. Believing that France had only suffered a temporary setback, he began to prepare an ambitious plan to conquer Russia. Napoleon envisioned the *Grande Armée* sweeping across the plains of Russia and occupying the Russian capital of Moscow. A victory over the Russian army would, he believed, force the czar to see reason and cooperate with him. The campaign, Napoleon hoped, would strengthen the Continental System, allow France permanent control in central Europe, and eventually bring England to its knees. But events would soon prove that Napoleon's penchant for underestimating his opponent could have fatal consequences.

# Underestimating the Enemy

**Chapter 4**

I N HIS IBERIAN CAMPAIGN, NAPOLEON had made a fatal mistake in underestimating a foe's determination to resist. Now, determined to humble the Russian czar once and for all and eliminate Russia's military threat to his control of central Europe, Napoleon was about to repeat that mistake on a grand scale. As it turned out, in his invasion of Russia Napoleon did more than underestimate his human foe. The vastness of Russia, as well as its primitive road system and brutal winter climate, would prove to be insurmountable challenges to the *Grande Armée*.

## France and Russia

Even before he physically invaded Russia, Napoleon signaled his hostile intentions with an attack on Russian trade. In 1810, Napoleon annexed the trading centers of Hamburg, Lubeck, and Bremen, and the Grand Duchy of Oldenburg, in what is now northern Germany. These ports had provided an important connection for Russian trade with England. The czar responded to Napoleon's move with a ukase, or imperial decree, announced on December 31, 1810, under which Russia placed high duties (taxes) on French goods and opened its own ports to English ships. Napoleon then countered by announcing that Poland now belonged to France. This was a direct challenge to the Russian czar, who considered himself the rightful ruler of the Polish nation.

Now Napoleon prepared once again for war with Russia. He intended to humble the czar on the battlefield and force Russia to recognize French dominion over Poland. French arms factories stepped up the manufacture of cannon and small arms, and a recruiting drive bolstered the French army. To his credit, Napoleon realized that this would be the most difficult military campaign of his career. He planned the attack carefully, but all the time disregarded the advice of his ambassador to Russia, Armand de Caulaincourt, who warned of the Russians' determination to resist him. In further preparation, Napoleon signed mutual defense treaties with Prussia (on February 24, 1812) and with Austria (on March 14, 1812). These agreements committed these two countries to contribute troops to fight alongside the *Grande Armée*.

In the meantime, the czar also prepared. Russia signed the Peace of Bucharest with the Ottoman Empire, temporarily ending a drawn-out military contest in southeastern Europe between the two empires. Russia reinforced its own army and its cavalry, which included a large contingent of Cossacks—skilled horsemen from the southern plains of Ukraine.

The Cossacks proved to be the French emperor's first miscalculation in his Russian campaign. Napoleon believed that he might

 **A Plot Against Napoleon Fails**

Napoleon had enjoyed the undying loyalty of the French nation since his first victories in the 1790s. But while campaigning in distant Russia, that loyalty began to unravel. During the retreat from Moscow, a plot against the emperor unfolded in Paris. The attempted coup was led by General Claude-Francois de Malet, an old revolutionary officer who had been confined to an asylum for conspiring against the government.

Malet escaped, proclaimed the death of Napoleon, and announced that France was once again a republic. He used forged documents to prove his assertions to police and military leaders. On October 23, 1812, Malet took control of Paris for several hours, ordering the arrest of the city's police minister, General Jean-Marie-Rene Savary. Malet then went to the home of the military governor of Paris, General Hulin, and killed the general with a pistol shot. Although army officers soon arrested Malet, uncovered his forgeries, and foiled his plot, the affair had the fateful consequence of showing that Napoleon's regime was not all-powerful and that the actions of a single man could, for a brief time, challenge the emperor's authority at the very center of his government.

persuade the Cossacks to fight alongside the French. But although the Cossacks regarded themselves as a sovereign nation and had fought many times for independence from Russia, they resisted France's attempts to enlist their help. Historian Philip Longworth reveals:

> [The French general] Murat attempted to rouse up [the Cossacks'] old anti-Tsarist feelings, but Cossacks rallied round the Tsar with a unanimity they had never shown before. Napoleon drew them all together—men of the [Cossack regions of] Kuban and the stormy Terek, of Orenburg and of the Ural. The whole of the quiet Don [River region] stirred, and when [Russian general Matvi Ivanovich] Platov called for volunteers, hoary veterans and boys barely in their teens flocked in to sacrifice themselves for Holy Russia.[22]

## Marching East

Despite the failure to enlist the Cossacks' help, in the spring of 1812 an immense procession of wagons, ammunition, and caissons pulled by more than three hundred thousand horses headed eastward from France through Germany and Poland. Napoleon himself left Paris on May 9, 1812, to take command of an army of more than six hundred thousand infantry and cavalry and about fourteen hundred artillery pieces. The army consisted of several nationalities, with Italians, Germans, Poles, Austrians, Swiss, Portuguese, and Spaniards making up important auxiliary forces.

Napoleon's assembly of this patchwork army was telling, as historian Michael Broers comments. "Napoleon's . . . need for allies more powerful than any he had previously called upon was ultimately a sign of weakness. Austria and Prussia were pressured into contributing troops for the campaign, a sign that the invasion of Russia was too big an undertaking for the states of the inner empire to tackle alone."[23]

While en route to Russia, Napoleon stopped in Dresden, the capital of Saxony. There, he had summoned the heads of state of Europe to meet with him and acknowledge him as their ruler. Napoleon needed to assure himself, in his own way, of their continuing loyalty to France and to him personally. Yet that loyalty was born not of friendship, but of fear. Historian J. Christopher Herold describes the scene:

> The emperor of Austria, the kings of Prussia, Saxony, Bavaria, Wurttemberg, Westphalia, and Naples; grand dukes, and dukes, and princes; field marshals and marshals of the Empire—all bowed before him and watched with terror and fascination as the stocky little man, pacing amidst the royal

*Napoleon's* Grande Armée, *consisting of six hundred thousand men, crosses the Nieman River en route to attack Russia.*

throng with a peculiar springy, soft, and pantherlike step, held forth like a bandit chief giving his final instructions before a robbery. Awe, admiration, hatred, and above all fear held them gripped. It is safe to wager that more than half those present, including his own marshals and ministers, wished that he were dead.[24]

On June 23, the *Grande Armée* crossed the Nieman River, the border between Russia and Poland. Napoleon had counted on the *Grande Armée* achieving a quick and decisive victory. With this in mind, the army reached the stronghold of Vilnius, in what was then the Russian province of Lithuania, on June 28. Much to Napoleon's surprise, however, the Russian army had evacuated Vilnius, leaving it an open city.

Confident that a single military victory would bring the czar to the negotiating table, Napoleon had not planned for the strategy his enemy had chosen: a steady retreat that drew the French forces deep into hostile territory. During the next weeks, the Russian army continued to withdraw and the French army followed, extending its lines of communication and supply ever further. As in Egypt and Spain, the French army was forced to live off the land, but the provisions that were available could not support such a huge force of men and horses. The lack of clean water brought dysentery and other debilitating sicknesses. Suffering illness, hunger, and homesickness, the French troops grew restless, thousands deserted. Without an answer to the Russian strategy of withdrawal, Napoleon pushed stubbornly ahead, still underestimating the Russian will to resist him.

For all his careful planning, Napoleon had failed to appreciate Russia's huge expanses. The size of the country made coordination between the different units of the *Grande Armée* difficult. Napoleon had also failed to take into account the lack of good roads. The uneven and potholed lanes which made up the Russian road network slowly destroyed the French wagons. Wheels sank in thick mud, and axles broke on the rutted roads. Artillery pieces had to be hauled forward by exhausted men and horses. An immense traffic jam extended for miles along the roads as the French horses, weakened by lack of food, began to die by the thousands.

Napoleon's underestimation of how Russia's vast distances would play havoc with logistics turned out to be the downfall of the

French army in Russia. Historian Richard K. Riehn summarizes the lessons Napoleon had failed to learn:

> The military machine Napoleon the artilleryman had created was perfectly suited to fight short, violent campaigns, but whenever a long-term sustained effort was in the offing, it tended to expose feet of clay. Napoleon had virtually invented mass armies. However, even though he knew how to wield these masses better than any man of his time, learning how to effectively support them in the field did not come nearly so easily. In the end, the logistics of the French military machine proved wholly inadequate.
>
> ... Napoleon's military machine ... had become an anachronism that could succeed only with the use of railroads and the telegraph. And these had not yet been invented.[25]

Historian Michael Broers comments on another important failure of Napoleon in Russia:

> Whereas Napoleon had clear political reasons for invading Russia, never before had he gone into war with such ill-defined military goals. In truth, the defined objectives of the campaign of 1812 did not extend much beyond catching a Russian army and defeating it in the field. Napoleon risked an interminable war [in Russia] in 1812, whether or not he succeeded in combat. Never before had he commanded so large a force over so vast an area and, at many crucial moments, it proved beyond him to adapt to these new demands.[26]

## Fighting at Smolensk and Borodino

As he had in the past, Napoleon blamed his commanders for the misfortune he had brought upon his army. Frustrated by the unwillingness of the Russians to fight, Napoleon turned on everyone around him, accusing them of misleading him into undertaking this campaign and of incompetence in carrying it out. Caulaincourt, the French ambassador to Russia, later recalled that:

> [Napoleon] was sure that we had deceived him personally about everything, down to the problems of the Russian cli-

mate, insisting that winter here was like that in France, except that it just lasted longer. These accusations against us were repeated on every occasion. I reiterated to the Emperor, quite in vain as it turned out, that I had not been exaggerating in the least, and that as his most faithful servant I had revealed the full truth about everything. But I failed to make him change his mind.[27]

In truth, Napoleon's bogged-down forces simply could not keep up with the Russian retreat—while Napoleon's criticism of his officers had the opposite effect of what the emperor had intended. Instead of inspiring his underlings to greater efforts, Napoleon's stinging rebukes were met with disloyalty and desertion.

*Russian troops stand against the* Grande Armée *at Borodino but fail to stop Napoleon's advance into the capital city of Moscow.*

Napoleon reserved his greatest anger for Czar Alexander, who failed to behave as Napoleon had predicted. Napoleon had believed that Alexander would conclude peace with him when he saw French troops overrunning his country. Alexander, however, had refused to bargain. Like many other European rulers, he was now determined to destroy Napoleon.

Not everything went against Napoleon, however. Thanks to disagreements between the Russian commanders, a planned Russian counterattack failed in early August. This allowed the French to cross the Dnieper River on August 13. The Russians withdrew to Smolensk, where a battle finally took place on August 17. The French bombarded the city, but a lack of cooperation among the French generals again prevented a decisive victory. When General Murat refused to allow Marshal Michel Ney's infantry to assist his own cavalry at the height of the battle, Murat's forces were mauled by a strong Russian division. The Battle of Smolensk, however, did force the Russians to withdraw and regroup farther east.

As the French approached Moscow, the Russian commanders decided to make a stand before the capital. On September 7, a huge battle took place at Borodino, a village on the Kalatsha River, the last town between Napoleon's army and Moscow, seventy miles to the east. Although they were outnumbered, the Russians managed to position themselves among the hills and forests east and south of the village and behind the steep banks of the Kalatsha River. Napoleon ordered a headlong drive straight into the center of the Russian line, but made a fatal error in placing his main artillery battery just out of range of the battlefield. Without artillery support, the French infantry was thrown back. The two sides fought for the rest of the day, with massive casualties on both sides. In the end, Napoleon forced the Russians back again, but at a terrible cost.

Napoleon had finally found the great battle he had been seeking for almost four months. However, one week later, on September 15, when the French army entered Moscow, it quickly became clear that this victory would be a hollow one. Nearly every single inhabitant, including the czar and his ministers, had fled the city, and the Kremlin Palace and fortification also stood empty. Still confident he would bring the czar to terms, Napoleon moved into Alexander's private apartments within the Kremlin.

Once again, Napoleon had underestimated Russian resolve. Not only had the Russians refused to negotiate, but they were also willing to ravage their own capital to deprive Napoleon of his prize. Soon after the French arrived, Russian troops and civilians set fires throughout the city. The Russians sabotaged water pumps and hoses, with the result that thousands of homes, churches, warehouses, and palaces burned to the ground. After the fire, French troops disobeyed orders against looting and sacked homes, shops, and marketplaces. The looting further depleted provisions and revealed an ominous breakdown of discipline within Napoleon's army.

Napoleon felt certain that the capture of the Russian capital would finally force the czar to conclude a peace agreement. But Alexander still refused to negotiate. He realized that Napoleon, instead of making a conquest, was now trapped deep inside Russia at the worst possible time. Winter was coming; Napoleon's long lines of supply and his escape routes were vulnerable to attack. There was no winter clothing for the French troops, and not enough horses to pull the artillery and supply wagons. Many wounded and sick soldiers were unable to move at all.

## The Winter Retreat

After spending a month in the deserted, smoldering Russian capital, Napoleon finally had to admit that the occupation of Moscow had gained him nothing. He ordered a retreat, which began on October 19 and which soon turned into a rout. Healthy soldiers struggled through mud, ice, and snow, in their haste leaving thousands of dead and wounded men by the wayside. Cossack cavalry harassed the columns by day, while wolves rampaged among the stragglers at night.

In the first week of November, the winter cold set in with a vengeance. By this time, the French army had turned into a disorganized rabble. After reaching Smolensk on November 9, the *Grande Armée* simply disintegrated. The Prussian and Bavarian commanders abandoned their men and returned home, while the Russians cut off the French escape route by occupying the city of Minsk, lying on the only road leading west out of Russia. Napoleon managed to get most of his army across the Berezina River, the last major physical barrier between his force and home, at the end of November. But the Russians cut off and captured thousands of French soldiers before they could make the crossing. Most of the French prisoners would soon die of hunger and cold.

Napoleon finally abandoned the army on December 5, putting Murat in charge of what remained of his forces—fewer than fifty thousand men, including a few thousand cavalry. The emperor of the French and master of Europe set off for Paris, disguised as Caulain-

## Napoleon Casts the Blame

*French soldiers extinguish flames as Moscow burns; Napoleon (wearing white pants) watches with disgust.*

Napoleon did not see his defeat in Russia as a failure of strategy but rather as a tactical setback, in which some minor miscalculations on his part brought about the final retreat. In his book *The Napoleonic Wars: An Illustrated History, 1792–1815*, historian Michael Glover quotes Napoleon on the campaign on Russia:

> It is the winter that has been our undoing. We are the victims of the climate. The fine weather [of the summer of 1812] tricked me. . . . Everything turned out badly because I stayed too long in Moscow. If I had left four days after I had occupied it, as I thought of doing when I saw it in flames, the Russians would have been lost. The Czar would gladly have accepted the terms I would have offered.

*Remnants of Napoleon's* Grande Armée *force their way across the Berezina River and out of Russia.*

court's secretary in order to pass safely through hostile territory in northern Germany. In the meantime, the Russians pursued the rest of Napoleon's army into Poland.

Historian Jacques Bainville describes the end result of the Russian campaign on Napoleon's army:

> When the Emperor left the Grand Army, its disintegration became complete, and it was "devil take the hindmost." Obedience was ended. Indiscipline spread even amongst the leaders. Everything was demoralized, and the spirit of defection was born. Murat, to whom the command had been entrusted, was not listened to, and he himself set a bad example. In the mud of Lithuania his only thoughts were for his kingdom [of Naples], his endangered crown, and once he openly treated his brother-in-law as a madman.[28]

The Russian campaign had been a complete disaster. Not only had Napoleon lost most of his army, he had transformed Czar Alexander into an implacable enemy who would not rest until

## A Quiet Arrival in Paris

As the French army struggled through snow and ice to return home in the late fall of 1812, Napoleon fled the scene of his defeat. Ordering a carriage to bring him back to France, he put on a disguise—posing as the secretary of his ambassador to Russia, Caulaincourt—to avoid capture by enemy troops. Napoleon and Caulaincourt traveled together and finally arrived at the gates of his palace, the Tuileries, in the dead of night, escorted by only a few horsemen.

The strange, almost comical arrival in Paris symbolized Napoleon's total defeat and humbling at the hands of the Russian army and its powerful allies: distance and climate. In his book *Napoleon Bonaparte*, historian Alan Schom includes Caulaincourt's description of the scene:

> The concierges [palace guardians] took us for some officers bearing dispatches and let us pass . . . the Swiss Guard, who had been asleep, came to the door in his nightshirt, a lantern in his hand, to see who was knocking. He was bewildered by our appearance and called his wife. I had to give my name several times before they agreed to open the door for us. He had to rub his eyes before he finally recognized us.

Napoleon was destroyed. Other nations under Napoleonic rule or occupation now regrouped for a campaign that would drive the French from central Europe and back across the Rhine River, the ancient border between France and Germany. The widespread fear of Napoleon's ability as a military commander disappeared, as the enemies of France now saw a greatly weakened French army and a leader who had made a terrible miscalculation.

Historian David Chandler, in the book *Napoleon and His Times,* describes this changed opinion of Napoleon among his enemies as the key result of the Russian campaign:

> The first result of the Russian Campaign was the irretrievable shattering of the legend of Napoleonic invincibility. Defeat in Russia, added to Britain's unquestioned command of the seas and the progressive deterioration of the Peninsular War . . . did much to build a new confidence among the governments and peoples of the submerged powers of continental Europe.[29]

# Choosing the Sword: Defeat in Germany

**Chapter 5**

**D**ESPITE THE HUMILIATING defeat in Russia, Napoleon still believed he held a strong hand, both militarily and economically, in Europe. He ignored the fact that all over the Continent, public opinion was turning against his empire. Napoleon's own driving ambition and thirst for military glory had brought about this reaction. The ideals of the French Revolution—the end of monarchy; justice; social and economic equality—had been replaced by the spirit of conquest. And despite the fact that Napoleon had brought important economic, legal, and social reforms to France, the rest of Europe resisted the Napoleonic vision. As described by the French historian Francois Furet in *Revolutionary France, 1770–1880:* "The French occupation's fiscal and military inroads formed the basis, in the long run, of general discontent: war nurtured war, and Napoleon's army became ever less French and ever more European, being drawn from the Grand Empire and the satellite states."[30]

## Unraveling Achievements

After the French retreat from Russia, Napoleon's diplomatic achievements began to unravel. It was plain to see that the emperor was vulnerable, unable to enforce the treaties he had made after his earlier victories. The states of Europe began to openly defy him. On December 30, 1812, the Prussian general Johann Yorck signed an armistice with Russia—without the consent of the Prussian king Frederick William III. This action unofficially ended Prussia's alliance with France. At first shocked by this news, Frederick William later went along with General Yorck. The king took heed of the rising patriotic

*Prussian king Frederick William III agreed to an armistice with Russia, effectively ending Prussia's alliance with France.*

fervor in Prussia and Napoleon's apparent weakness, and he made peace with the czar. Of this important new alliance, military historian Albert Sidney Britt III writes: "The political consequences of Yorck's defiant 'disobedience' were immense. Although Frederick William repudiated his action, it is clear that Yorck's deed emboldened him to make the final break with Napoleon. The very soul of Prussia was stirred, in turn putting more pressure on the Government to cast off the French yoke."[31]

Napoleon did not heed the serious danger that the Prussian king's action represented. He believed he could still count on Austria and on the Austrian emperor, Francis I, whose daughter, Marie-Louise, Napoleon had married in 1810. Here, a diplomatic strategy founded on a marriage alliance also failed. Austria followed Prussia's example by signing its own armistice with the Russians, abandoning the alliance with France. Historian J. Christopher Herold writes of Napoleon's naive belief in the Austrian alliance:

> Even the most hardened realists have blind spots of naivete, and Napoleon was no exception. There can be little doubt that he had seriously held on to the belief that Emperor Francis of Austria would never make war on the husband of his daughter, notwithstanding abundant historical examples of such base behavior. The sudden realization of Austria's du-

plicity cured him of his dynastic delusions and filled him with anguish.[32]

Despite the setbacks he had experienced, Napoleon would not retreat from the rest of Europe. As Albert Sidney Britt III continues: "The campaign of 1812 was over, and Napoleon had failed in a colossal misadventure. But it was clear that the struggle for Europe was far from finished. Napoleon's return to Paris was no admission of defeat, but rather a statement of his intention to raise a new army."[33]

Napoleon believed that he could never abandon the conquests that France had made in the 1790s: the capture of the west bank of the Rhine, the defeat of the Austrians in northern Italy, and the extension of French dominance into Belgium. Napoleon saw these conquests as a point of personal honor, the key to his popularity. Were he to lose them, he feared the empire he had created would fall.

## A Show of Strength

In the meantime, English armies and Spanish guerrillas were driving the French army from Spain. The Portuguese capital of Lisbon was in English hands, giving Napoleon's enemy a deepwater port that English ships could use without any interference from the French navy. Four years of guerrilla warfare had drained France of troops and money, while Napoleon refused to admit defeat and retreat.

Napoleon realized that his defeat in Spain would make his enemies even more determined to reconquer other territory lost to the *Grande Armée*. He believed that Britain would now demand the surrender of Belgium, and that Prussia, which had just invaded the French-controlled kingdom of Saxony in what is now central Germany, would drive all the way to the Rhine.

Napoleon realized that his army could not face a coalition of Austria, Russia, and Prussia on the field of battle and survive. Yet he believed the only solution to his dilemma was to throw his armies back into Germany in a show of strength. Once again, he depended on his skill as a military leader to defeat his rivals. Historian Britt writes: "Spanish, British, Germans, and Russians now threatened his Continental System. After another frustrating year of fighting the elusive foe in Spain, he decided on a final solution to his predicament—he would march eastwards in quest of one more decisive battle. Once more the Emperor would entrust the fate of his Empire to the sword."[34]

As in the past, Napoleon saw conquest as necessary before diplomacy. He had always refused to deal from a weak position, negotiating only after establishing his military superiority. His strategy was to defeat the Allies on the battlefield, then use conquered German territories as buffers between his empire and Russia and Prussia. He drafted another army of conscripts, then led the revived, but much smaller, *Grande Armée* back across the Rhine. During this campaign of 1813, the French fought Prussian and Russian armies at the Battles of Lutzen and Bautzen. These battles ended in draws, but Napoleon proclaimed a great victory in a speech designed to boost the morale of his troops:

> Soldiers, I am pleased with you! You have fulfilled my expectations! You have achieved everything by your readiness to obey and by your courage. On the famous 2nd of May you defeated and routed the Russian and Prussian armies, commanded by the Emperor Alexander and the King of Prussia. You have added a new lustre to the glory of my eagles. . . .

*An artistic depiction shows the marriage of Napoleon and Austrian Marie-Louise.*

> We shall hurl back these Tartars [Russians] to their horrible
> climate, which they must never leave. Let them stay in their
> icy deserts, the abode of slavery, barbarity and corruption,
> where man is debased to the level of the brute.[35]

After these inconclusive battles, Napoleon signed the Armistice
of Plesswitz with Austria. Napoleon wanted to keep Austria neutral
while he dealt with the threat from Prussia and Russia. Yet despite
his military and diplomatic maneuvers, what he most feared was
still coming about: a general coalition of all the European powers
against him. Later that month, Prussia, England, and Russia signed
the Treaty of Reichenbach. This treaty held that all of these allies
must agree on the terms of peace to be made with France. It had the
effect of uniting the three powers in their common goal of defeating Napoleon and returning France to its old boundaries.

It became increasingly clear that the alliance Napoleon had made
with Austria through his marriage with Marie-Louise had been a failure. Austria was preparing to maneuver itself into an open break with
Napoleon by setting peace terms that the emperor was bound to re-
ject. The strategy adopted by the Allies was to appear reasonable but
to deliberately provoke Napoleon to make war again. This, the Allied
leaders believed, would bring the French people, exhausted by years
of war and sacrifice, into an open breach with their emperor.

## The Battle of Leipzig

Napoleon's insatiable military ambition played directly into the
Allied strategy. Realizing that an important showdown in central
Europe was coming, the Allies coordinated their forces and their
strategy, which was to always retreat when Napoleon himself was
present but to stand and fight against Napoleon's generals when the
emperor was absent. They also intended to play for time and force
the French to fight a long, exhausting campaign far from their home
and base of supply. Albert Sidney Britt III notes that: "News of
French problems in supply and morale indicated that the [battles]
fought in August had . . . weakened Napoleon's army. Time was
clearly working against the Emperor. Only a great battle could
solve his strategic problem. . . . Napoleon would be destroyed, not
by a great battle, but by attrition."[36]

## Napoleon's Tactics Fail

Napoleon Bonaparte's innovation in the art of war was to make it mobile. He avoided the usual set battles, in which two sides of formed-up units simply came to a halt and fire at each other until one side broke. Instead, Napoleon maneuvered his forces to take advantage of terrain, of the enemy's weak spots, and of the element of surprise. He always sought either to turn the enemy flank or hit the rear of the enemy line. He attacked the crucial point in the enemy position that, if overrun, would send the defending forces into a full-scale retreat.

Napoleon called this strategy the *attaque tournante*, or turning attack. This strategy was best used when he had superior forces, which could maneuver without fear of an effective enemy counterattack. But when faced with an enemy army equal to or larger than his own, the *attaque tournante* proved a bad idea. Napoleon was not as skilled at defensive strategy or at carrying out an ordinary, set battle. This was a crucial reason for defeats when he was outnumbered: in Germany in 1813 and at Waterloo in 1815.

Napoleon finally collected his army on the plains of Saxony, determined to draw the Allies into a decisive engagement. On October 16, 1813, the battle finally began near the city of Leipzig. Historians have nicknamed the three-day Battle of Leipzig the "Battle of the Nations," as the forces of all the principal Napoleonic-era states, except for England, took part. The two sides fought to a stalemate until the third day, when Napoleon's Saxon allies turned against the emperor, transforming the stalemate into a rout of the French. The French army fell back to the west. Soon afterward, Jerome Bonaparte was driven out of the kingdom of Westphalia, and the Allies, now in control of Gemany, officially dissolved the Confederation of the Rhine, the coalition of states Napoleon had assembled to protect France from her rivals in central Europe. Napoleon retreated across the Rhine and reached the French garrison of Mainz on November 2. He entered the city of Saint-Cloud on November 9.

Napoleon's monarchy, the state known by historians as the First Empire, was doomed at the Battle of Leipzig, which also destroyed his prestige at home. Neither diplomacy nor warfare could save him now. Historian Francois Furet describes the emperor's predicament:

> Napoleon found himself on the Rhine with the debris of his
> army, and France threatened on its oldest frontiers.

But this time, it was a weary France, broken by despotism and hazardous undertakings, a country of discontented notables, tired marshals and revolutionaries grown old. Napoleon might well be able to get his new conscripts . . . to perform a few strategic feats, but he could no longer mobilize any national force to counterbalance, either in number or will to win, the formidable enemy coalition.[37]

## An Exhausted France

Once again, the *Grande Armée* of the French Empire had been destroyed. The French army had suffered seventy thousand casualties at the Battle of Leipzig. During the retreat after the battle, Napoleon

*Allied forces clash with the* Grande Armée *at the Battle of Leipzig, ultimately killing seventy thousand French soldiers and further weakening the emperor's authority in France.*

# The French Change Their Loyalty

*Russian czar Alexander and Prussian king Frederick lead the Allies to Paris amidst throngs of excited French citizens.*

A contemporary description of the triumphant entry of the Allies into Paris on March 30, given in Michael Glover's book *The Napoleonic Wars*, shows that the people of France were by now sick and tired of Napoleon Bonaparte and ready to pledge their allegiance elsewhere.

> [The Russian czar and the king of Prussia] entered the barrier of Paris about 11 o'clock, the Cossacks of the Guard forming the advance of the march. Already was the crowd so enormous, as well as the acclamations so great, that it was difficult to move forward. . . . All Paris seemed to be assembled and concentrated on one spot. They thronged in such masses round the emperor and king that with all their condescending and gracious familiarity, extending their hands on all sides, it was vain to attempt to satisfy the populace; they were positively eaten up amidst the cries of "Vive l'empereur Alexandre! Vive le roi de Prusse! Vive nos liberateurs!" Nor did the air alone resound with these peals for, with louder acclamations, if possible, they were mingled with those of "Vive le roi! Vive Louis XVIII! Vive les Bourbons! Bas le tyran!"

lost more than ten thousand men to desertion, capture, and disease, while most of the German soldiers fighting in his army slipped away and returned to their homes.

By the time Napoleon reached the Rhine River, about sixty thousand soldiers remained, out of an army numbering several hundred thousand at the beginning of the campaign. This time, the emperor would not recover. There was no money left in the French treasury to rebuild the army, and the territories forced to pay tribute in central Europe were now under the control of the Allies. The Russians had thrown the emperor back; the English had triumphed in Spain; the Allies had reached the Rhine—and this time, they would not stop at the frontiers of France. The Prussian general Gneiseneau, for one, was determined to crush Napoleon and his empire once and for all:

> We must take revenge for the many sorrows inflicted upon the nations, and for so much arrogance. If we do not, then we are miserable wretches indeed, and deserve to be shocked out of our lazy peace every two years and threatened with the scourge of slavery. . . . We must return the visits of the French to our cities, by visiting them in theirs. Until we do, our revenge and triumph will be incomplete. If the Silesian [Prussian] Army reaches Paris first, I shall at once have the bridges of Austerlitz and Jena blown up, as well as the Arc de Triomphe.[38]

By this time the French were completely fed up with war and with the ambitious Napoleon Bonaparte. No longer in fear of the emperor, the French legislature demanded that he make peace immediately. Napoleon responded by accusing all his adversaries of conspiring to bring back the Bourbon monarchy. In fact, he was correct—many of the legislative deputies were seeking to return the Bourbons to the throne. Their purpose was to bring a weary France some degree of peace and stability after more than twenty years of revolution, political chaos, and war.

Napoleon would not admit his mistakes. Instead, he believed that he had been poorly served by his generals and by the members of his family. But his generals saw clearly that France could not keep up the war against the Allies. One by one, they deserted Napoleon to ally themselves with the Bourbon claimant, Louis XVIII. Having lost all support within France, on January 25, 1814, Napoleon abandoned Paris. In a desperate attempt to keep his dynasty alive, he appointed Marie-Louise as regent for his son and named his brother Joseph Bonaparte as lieutenant general of the empire.

The Allies continued their advance on Paris. On March 3, the garrison of Soissons, just north of the capital, surrendered. Paris fell to the Allies later that month, on March 30, as Marie-Louise and

*In the palace at Fontainebleau in April of 1814, Napoleon's marshals plead with the emperor to abdicate.*

Joseph fled. On April 2, the Senate voted to overthrow Napoleon, who was finally confronted by his general staff on April 4 at his palace of Fontainebleau. The generals demanded his abdication, which Napoleon finally offered on April 7, 1814. The emperor's response was indicative of his instinctive reliance on war to accomplish his aims: "Neither you nor the army need shed any more blood. Resign yourselves to living under the Bourbons and to serving them faithfully. You wanted peace, now you can have it. But the peace that you long for will destroy more of you as you lie in your feather-beds than war would have done in our bivouacs."[39]

Marie-Louise and Napoleon's son returned to Vienna, where they remained. The rest of the Bonaparte family scattered into exile.

Napoleon agreed to exile himself to the island of Elba, lying off the coast of Italian Tuscany. He was then escorted under guard to the Mediterranean port of Frejus. During the trip angry peasants and townspeople attacked his carriage; Napoleon also saw himself burned in effigy. He wore disguises, including an Austrian uniform, to escape through Provence, a territory that had always resisted the authority of the central government in distant Paris and which now was openly hostile to Napoleon. On April 27, Napoleon boarded the HMS *Undaunted*, a British frigate, and set sail for Elba, where he landed on May 4, 1814. Napoleon was now the emperor of only a small island.

In fear of assassination, Napoleon had demanded a guardian. The English had agreed and appointed Sir Neil Campbell, whose mission was to keep watch on the emperor and assure that he remained isolated and powerless. Still seeking what glory he might, however, Napoleon immediately took possession of the nearby island of Pianosa, which had been abandoned five years earlier. On Elba, he issued decrees on the cultivation of land and ordered the construction of new roads, to be built by laborers conscripted from the villages and paid for by new taxes.

Meanwhile, the brother of Louis XVI returned to France and was proclaimed King Louis XVIII. By the Treaty of Paris, signed on May 30, 1814, France was reduced to the frontiers of 1792. The Allied powers then convened the Congress of Vienna to forge a new international agreement in the wake of the Napoleonic Wars.

In the meantime, on the island of Elba, Napoleon still found himself unable to accept his final defeat. He believed that many French

people still supported him, still sought to keep the gains of the Revolution, and still detested the Bourbon dynasty. He still considered
the French army to be unstoppable and the Allied coalition to be
weak and indecisive. For nearly a year, Napoleon plotted a triumphant return to France, and one final great battle that he hoped
would restore him to his rightful place as emperor of the French and
the most powerful man in Europe.

# A Failure of Perception: Defeat at Waterloo

**Chapter 6**

FOR ALL HIS BRILLIANCE in military strategy, Napoleon often failed in his perception of his own situation and prospects in his assessment of others. He was a supremely gifted egotist who considered all others as inferior to himself and therefore likely to submit to his will. Nor did he trouble himself over his own army's limits of endurance. In Egypt, he had not bothered to plan for the difficulties his soldiers encountered in a hot desert, far from their homeland. In Spain, he had disregarded the Spaniards' will to fight occupation by the French. In Russia, he ignored the problems of supply and distance and had underestimated Russian resistance. He had not understood Emperor Francis's resentment of French military victories over the armies of Austria, nor did he believe the English could outmaneuver the Continental System.

By the time of his exile on Elba, Napoleon accepted the fact that the Allies had struck an important blow against his First Empire. Yet he still believed he had a chance to regain the confidence of the French, to outmaneuver the Allies, and return to power. As long as he was alive, he could not admit defeat, nor could he accept life as a powerless exile on a poor and meaningless island. Increasingly deluded by his past triumphs and glories, he came to believe that the French people sought his return and the overthrow of the king. Francois Furet describes Napoleon's impatience:

> The island of Elba was badly guarded, France vaguely uneasy, the great man disconsolate in his tiny kingdom of exile. He had kept intact that power of imagination and action which set him apart from the rest of humanity. He had never

*The French garrison at Grenoble welcomes Napoleon (pictured on horse)*
*back to France after fleeing the island of Elba.*

stopped putting back on the table the stakes accumulated by
his victories, even when those stakes were too awesome to
be reasonably gambled again. On the isle of Elba, he had
nothing left to play with but his tireless genius and the magic
of memories. The historian is astounded that the allies, who
had for so long watched him risk everything when he had
everything to lose, could not have foreseen more clearly that
he would still try to regain everything now that he no longer
had anything to lose.[40]

On February 26, 1815, while Governor Campbell was visiting his mistress on the mainland of Italy, Napoleon escaped the island of Elba with a flotilla of seven vessels and several hundred followers, who had assembled to help the emperor reconquer France. On March 1, the flotilla anchored in the Golfe Juan, on the Mediterranean coast of France. The emperor marched his tiny force to the port of Cannes. From there he proceeded into the mountains lying to the north, toward the town of Grenoble. While on Elba, he had smuggled letters to the commander of the Grenoble garrison, Colonel Charles de la Bedoyere. Loyal to Napoleon, this officer marched his troops out of the city to welcome Napoleon and to throw in his lot with the returning emperor.

On March 10, Napoleon entered Lyon, where soldiers and civilians greeted him with enthusiasm. He continued toward Paris, marching through the eastern French region of Burgundy. Uncertain of how to stop this gathering force, Louis XVIII sent three separate armies against Napoleon. But mass desertion weakened these forces while the officers found themselves unable to organize and coordinate their units. On March 20, after Marshal Ney defected from the king's army, Louis fled the capital, leaving Paris open to Napoleon's forces.

In this case, Napoleon was partly correct in his assessment of the situation. He sensed that the people of France sought to avenge the humiliation of their nation by the Allies and the loss of territory in eastern France, Belgium, and Italy. Many had no love for the Bourbon monarchy, recalling the tyranny and injustice they had suffered under the old regime. Most wanted to save the social and political progress made by the Revolution—and saw Napoleon as their best hope to achieve this and get rid of the Bourbons for good.

What Napoleon failed to appreciate was the determination of the Allies to keep the French west of the Rhine and turn back the tide of revolutionary change that Napoleon had unleashed on Europe. The Allied monarchs were determined to defeat what they considered dangerous republicanism and maintain the status quo of monarchy and the imperial state. To reduce the threat from the troublesome French, the monarchs of England, Austria, Prussia, and Russia wanted Napoleon back in exile and France powerless to mount any more grand campaigns. To achieve this, the Allies once again formed a coalition of armies to meet and defeat Napoleon.

# A Wit Observes Napoleon

Historian David Hamilton-Williams, in *The Fall of Napoleon*, quotes one Parisian satirist who observed the ever-changing attitudes of the French people toward their returning emperor:

The Tiger has broken out of his cage.

The Ogre has been three days at sea.

The Wretch has landed at Frejus.

The Buzzard has reached Antibes.

The Invader has arrived at Grenoble.

The General has entered Lyons.

Napoleon slept at Fontainebleau last night.

The Emperor will proceed to the Tuileries today.

His Imperial Majesty will address his loyal subjects tomorrow.

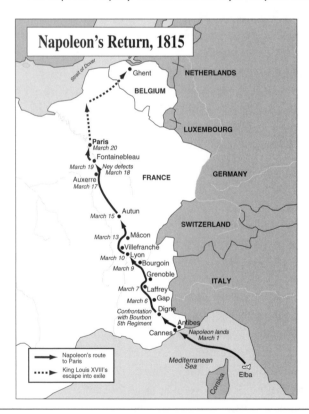

## A New Constitution

Napoleon ordered all those loyal to the Bourbons to leave the capital and declared a new constitution that abolished press censorship and removed Catholicism as the state religion (which Louis XVIII, during his brief reign, had established). Napoleon believed that these reforms would bring him renewed popularity at home. At the same time, he hoped to convince the Allies that he no longer represented a threat to them.

Still, Napoleon overestimated the depth of his support. Although many ordinary people, remembering the glory of his past conquests, still supported the emperor, members of the clergy, the old landowning nobility, and many government officials openly defied him. Millions of families had lost sons, husbands, and brothers as a result of the various military campaigns Napoleon had mounted. Throughout France, nearly everyone wished only for peace.

Meanwhile, the Allies gathered their forces. On March 25, the Treaty of Vienna was signed by Britain, Austria, Russia, and Prussia. By this agreement, the Allies combined their armies to oppose Napoleon. The Allies now realized that a final, decisive defeat of Napoleon had become a dire necessity. There could be no peace or agreement, according to historian David Hamilton-Williams:

> War was now inevitable. [The British government] would not countenance peace with Napoleon; to do so in their view would mean having to keep Britain on a permanent war footing. Not only that, but a weak, subservient, even dependent, Bourbon throne [in France] would suit Britain's trading interests. . . .
>
> Napoleon had hoped that with his "bloodless" return . . . aided by virtually the entire population, his offer of constitutional monarchy and acceptance of the old French borders would induce the Powers to allow him to rule France in peace.[41]

## Playing for Time

Napoleon believed he could play for time while his armies assembled. Through ambassador Caulaincourt, he tried to contact the Allied governments and come to some kind of accommodation. He ignored the fact that his past military conquests had made implacable enemies of every major government in Europe.

   The Allies steadfastly refused to settle or meet with Napoleon. Realizing this, the emperor began making plans for his next campaign. This time, his goal was to destroy the British and Prussian armies threatening France from what had once been French-controlled territory in Belgium. He believed that once an adequate French army was in the field, his superior generalship would overcome the Allies, despite the fact that his forces would be outnumbered. In *Men of Waterloo*, author John Sutherland describes the emperor's grandiose plan for final victory:

## Preparing for Waterloo

In *The Fall of Napoleon*, historian David Hamilton-Williams gives the following description of France's frenzied preparation for Napoleon's last campaign against the Allies:

> Napoleon had mobilized the nation for war, and his and the nation's needs were great. . . . Imperial factories opened all over the country on Napoleon's order for 235,000 muskets with bayonets, and 15,000 pairs of pistols. The great cutlery manufacturers of Moulins and the Langres took on hundreds of employees on day and night shifts to produce bayonets and swords. In Paris and all over France, tailors, seamstresses and clothiers set up factories to produce uniforms, Paris alone turning out 1,250 uniforms a day. Tanners, leather craftsmen, cobblers and glove-makers combined to produce 195,000 pairs of boots, leather equipment, harness and other horse equipment. Thousands were employed in the manufacture of munitions. At Vincennes, 12,000,000 cartridges were produced by hand in two months, this involving paper manufacture, gunpowder production and the moulding of musket ball.

Although the factories and workshops worked at full tilt, they had the promise of pay for their efforts. Napoleon's mobilization of troops for the battlefield was much less successful. An entire generation had already been fighting for the emperor, and French families were no longer so willing to make the sacrifice of their sons and husbands. The majority of new conscripts simply stayed at home, and Napoleon mustered less than half of the five hundred thousand troops he believed he needed to challenge and defeat the Allies in the upcoming campaign.

Success in Belgium just might bring down the allies like a stack of cards, the Emperor believed. With [Arthur Wellesley, now the duke of] Wellington crushed, the British government might fall. This could mean that a peace party would take over England, and Britain could come out of the military picture for months to come. [The Prussian general] Blucher, if he lived, would straggle back to Prussia. Then with the forces the French picked up in Belgium, Napoleon would move against the Russian and Austrian armies. Most of the troops he had left on the French frontiers would be part of his victorious army. There would be reinforcements from garrisons and new trainees. He could destroy the Russians and pin down the Austrians by threatening Vienna. Finally, with only the Austrians on the field, total victory would be his.[42]

Not only did Napoleon seriously underestimate the resolve of the Allies to crush him once and for all, he also overestimated the ability of France to undertake another war. The treasury was nearly empty, and the government could not clothe or arm most of its troops. The conscription drive raised less than half the troops he had decided were needed to prevail against the Allies. Many formerly loyal generals refused to serve under Napoleon, instead fleeing to foreign countries in support of the exiled king. As a consequence, while the Allies assembled nearly 750,000 men, Napoleon's northern army included only about 300,000.

On June 12, 1815, Napoleon left Paris, traveling northward toward Belgium. His plan was to split the British and Prussian forces, defeat them one by one, and capture the Belgian capital of Brussels. But the campaign started off badly, as missed orders and poor coordination threw the French army into chaos. Napoleon reached the town of Charleroi on June 15, but the French general Bourmont then defected to the Prussians, bringing with him Napoleon's battle plan.

## The Final Defeat at Waterloo

Napoleon continued due north toward Brussels, which was protected by an English army under General Wellington. Napoleon had yet to realize that he was marching with generals who would no longer give him the unconditional support and untiring effort he had once enjoyed.

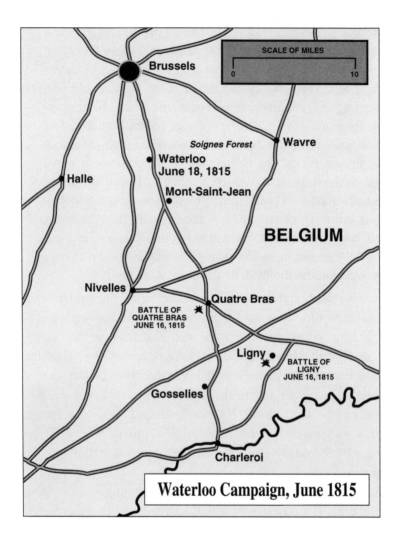

**Waterloo Campaign, June 1815**

When Marshal Michel Ney, one of Napoleon's most experienced and capable officers, marched against the crossroads town of Quatre Bras, he stopped and did not advance against the English. Napoleon then ordered Ney to withdraw and attack the Prussians, who were advancing from the east. These instructions infuriated the headstrong Ney, who instead ordered a suicidal cavalry attack against the English infantry. The French troops were thrown back with heavy losses.

At the same time, Napoleon lacked good intelligence on the enemy position and numbers. Still overconfident, he believed he really had no need for this information and that his tactical skill would overcome the Allied superiority in numbers. For a brief time, it seemed that events would prove Napoleon correct. Discovering that the Prussian army had formed a long front to the northeast, he ordered an attack eastward against the Prussian flank. This maneuver ended with intensive fighting around the town of Ligny on June 16. After the Prussian general Gebhard Blucher was thrown from his horse, the Prussian army turned away from the battlefield in an orderly retreat.

On June 17, Wellington withdrew from Quatre Bras northward to Mont-Saint-Jean, lining his forces up with Blucher's, ten miles to the east. In the meantime, poor communications worked against Napoleon. Messengers failed to bring news from the battlefronts or arrived with information that was too old to be useful. Conflicting reports from Quatre Bras and Ligny led Napoleon into believing that Ney had defeated and thrown back Wellington's forces and that the Prussian army was retreating out of Belgium.

Assuming he had defeated his opponents, Napoleon failed to reconnoiter the battlefield, and so learned too late that the Prussians had made an orderly retreat and that Wellington had held fast before Ney's army. In any case, Napoleon believed that he had to strike a crushing blow as soon as possible, rather than hold his position. Early in the afternoon on June 16, he marched to Quatre Bras and ordered an immediate attack on the English.

Now the weather became a factor in the Allies' favor. A heavy rainstorm broke out, turning the roads muddy. The poor conditions slowed the French advance and made it harder for infantry and cavalry to maneuver into position. The storm also allowed the English time to take up a strong defensive position around Mont-Saint-Jean. Wellington waited for the attack, realizing that time and the weather were now both on his side.

The main battle of Waterloo took place on June 18, 1815. The battle began around noon, with Napoleon ordering his brother Jerome to lead his troops to the farm of Hougoumont, lying between the French and English lines. Napoleon planned to break the English line in two and drive Wellington back toward Brussels. Hougoumont farm became the scene of intense close-quarters combat as English troops repulsed wave after wave of charges by the French infantry.

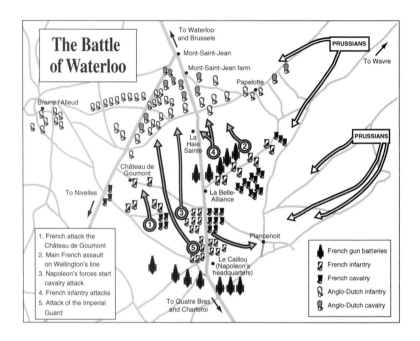

The Battle of Waterloo

To Waterloo and Brussels

Mont-Saint-Jean

PRUSSIANS

To Wavre

Mont-Saint-Jean farm

Papelotte

Braine l'Alleud

PRUSSIANS

La Haie Sainte

Château de Goumont

To Nivelles

La Belle-Alliance

Plancenoit

1. French attack the Château de Goumont
2. Main French assault on Wellington's line
3. Napoleon's forces start cavalry attack
4. French infantry attacks
5. Attack of the Imperial Guard

Le Caillou (Napoleon's headquarters)

To Quatre Bras and Charleroi

French gun batteries
French infantry
French cavalry
Anglo-Dutch infantry
Anglo-Dutch cavalry

Gradually, the English troops defending Hougoumont weakened before the French assaults. At one point, French and English soldiers were firing at each other through the doors and windows of the farmhouse and outbuildings. During this pivotal moment, General Blucher and the Prussians were spotted marching toward the battlefield from the east. Napoleon sent a messenger to General Emmanuel de Grouchy, on the French right (eastern) flank, ordering Grouchy to attack Blucher's force. In the rain and mud, the messenger took four hours to reach his destination, while Grouchy began a march toward the town of Wavre—which Blucher had left behind.

## Calling on Marshal Ney

In the meantime, the English decimated the French lines with musket fire at the farm of La Haie Sainte, lying just northeast of Hougoumont. Napoleon ordered Marshal Ney to make a cavalry charge on the farm, but a force of German troops under Wellington's command threw Ney back. Ney then ordered a charge of his cavalry troops against the strongest point of the English line. The result was the same as at Quatre Bras two days earlier. The massed English infantry poured their bullets and musket balls directly into the charging horsemen, at some points firing point-blank, while an intense artillery bombardment that Napoleon had previously ordered against this part of the line killed many more French horsemen.

At this point, Napoleon's failure to correctly assess those serving him became critical. Napoleon knew Marshal Ney as one of his best cavalry commanders, but had not counted on Ney's stubbornness and willful disregard for the lives of his troops. The suicidal cavalry charge on La Haie Sainte ended in a complete rout, as the French survivors struggled desperately to retreat from the carnage. According to historian James Marshall-Cornwall: "Napoleon . . . handed over to Ney the whole conduct of the attack—a fatal error. Ney's gallantry in action was unchallenged, but he was headstrong and wayward, with little tactical sense."[43]

---

*Allied British highlanders stand in square formation against repeated French cavalry charges during the Battle of Waterloo.*

The attack weakened, but did not break, the English lines. In the meantime, the Prussian army approached the battlefield, forcing back the outnumbered and exhausted French units sent to stop them. Instead of retreating, Napoleon ordered fresh attacks on La Haie Sainte. Ney then attacked Wellington again with the elite Imperial Guard—troops hand-selected for their bravery, skill, and loyalty to Napoleon—while the emperor ordered another artillery barrage. Once again, the English forced their adversaries to retreat in disarray. At the terrifying sight of the Imperial Guard in a total panic, the French army began a disorderly retreat from the battlefield. Author John Sutherland describes the scene:

> *"Le Garde recule!"* ["The Guard retreats!"] was a shout of doom. Troops on the right screamed it and pointed in disbelief to the Imperial Guardsmen as they streaked away. . . . There was panic. It began with the first shouts and then snowballed into unbelievable proportions. There were still units on the field who had not seen the debacle. But they were like mounds of dry sand in front of a raging torrent. For the moment they kept up the heavy fire against the British. The word triggered a heavy retreat by the French troops engaged with the Prussians who had just joined Wellington's left flank. They flew in disorder. As Napoleon watched from La Haye Sainte he could see his whole empire cascading down the heights, for it was the Guard which held his last measure of power.[44]

Finally, Napoleon had to accept the fact that his army was beaten. With his Imperial Guard in full flight from the field of Waterloo, the emperor turned back toward France, away from the surging English and Prussian armies. He left behind his train of coaches, which carried gold, jewelry, private papers, and other valuables—the bulk of his personal fortune. The coaches became the target of frenzied soldiers and local farmers who swarmed around the imperial carriages to loot and destroy them. Napoleon gave no orders before his retreat from the battlefield. Ney, Grouchy, and the other remaining French commanders abandoned their troops and fled as well.

Napoleon reached Paris on June 21. Once again, however, he refused to admit that his was a lost cause. In a letter to his ministers, he had written:

> I believe the Deputies will be made to understand that it is their duty to join me in saving France. . . . All is not lost by

## French and British Tactics

The armies of the eighteenth century drew on both trained, professional soldiers—who knew how to fight in disciplined lines—and untrained draftees, who had a much lesser ability to march, turn, and obey orders in unison. The difference in experience and training brought about different tactics on the battlefield, and this difference provided a key to the outcome of the contest between English and French units at the Battle of Waterloo. As described by historian Michael Glover in his book *The Napoleonic Wars:*

> The scale of conscripted [drafted] armies raised tactical problems. The linear tactics of the eighteenth century necessitated a very high standard of training which could not be drilled into hastily raised recruits. Other methods of achieving victory had to be devised and, more from necessity than conviction, the French put their faith in shock action rather than firepower. They subordinated everything in the attempt to rupture the opposing line by bursting through it with a mass of men ready to accept heavy casualties (which could be replaced by conscription) and determined to achieve a crushing victory. This technique proved highly successful (especially against under-trained troops fighting in line) and, in combination with other factors . . . made the armies of Napoleon the model for every other army in Europe, with one exception. The exception was Britain which, having no conscription, could not afford to adopt tactics which demanded heavy casualties.

The remarkable stand of the English infantry before wave after wave of French assaults and cavalry charges decided the outcome on June 18, 1815, the fateful last day of Waterloo and the last day of battle Napoleon would ever see.

a long chalk. . . . I shall call up one hundred thousand conscripts. The federes and the National Guard will provide another one hundred thousand men. . . . I can call up a levee en masse in Dauphine, at Lyons, in Burgundy, Lorraine and Champagne. . . . I shall soon have three hundred thousand soldiers under arms with which to face the enemy! Then I'll simply crush them once and for all![45]

On hearing the news of the defeat at Waterloo, the Chamber of Representatives convened. On June 22, the chamber sent an ultimatum to Napoleon to abdicate immediately. With his support in the legislature gone and his army defeated, Napoleon finally had to admit that there was no way to salvage his government. He issued a proclamation in which he officially resigned and turned over his title of emperor of the French to his son as Napoleon II.

The British and Prussians drove south from Belgium, with no French army to stop them. On November 20, 1815, the representatives of the French government and the Allies signed the Treaty of Paris. Under this agreement, France surrendered all of the territory it had won since the Revolution and was ordered to pay an indemnity of seven hundred million francs.

## The Final Retreat

By the time the treaty was signed, Napoleon was already in exile. The emperor had planned to leave France and take refuge in the United States and in early July had asked that two French ships anchored off the Atlantic coast prepare to receive him. On July 8, Napoleon was rowed out to a French frigate, *La Salle*, but the English warship *Bellerophon* blocked the port and the emperor's escape, and its captain ordered Napoleon aboard his ship. Napoleon obeyed on July 15. He was transported to England, then put aboard the *Northumberland*, which sailed for the tiny island of Saint Helena, in the South Atlantic Ocean.

On Saint Helena, Napoleon had the rest of his life to reflect on his past and on the great changes he had wrought in France and Europe. He dictated his memoirs, idled in his rooms, cultivated a small garden, and bickered with the guardians appointed to watch over him. Finally, after a long illness, he died on May 5, 1821.

To the end, Napoleon saw himself as a man of the people—someone who had risen by ability and ambition, and not by rank or privilege. Without noble titles, born on distant, poor Corsica, and trained as nothing more than a humble officer of artillery, he had managed to rise to great power and make himself, for a few years, the master of Europe. He was the first product of a new France, and his career was one of the most important results of the French Revolution, which swept away the old aristocracy and the Bourbon monarchy and promised the French people liberty, equality, and fraternity. On August 27, 1816, while speaking with the author B. E. O'Meara, Napoleon offered a story to demonstrate what he believed his life had really meant:

*A dejected Napoleon stands aboard the English warship* Bellerophon *after the former French emperor's escape to the United States was blockaded.*

On my return from Elba I saw an old woman hobbling along with the help of a crutch. I was not recognised. "Well, *ma bonne*, and where are you going?" "*Ma foi*," replied the old dame, "they tell me the emperor is here, and I want to see him before I die." "Bah," said I, "what do you want to see him for? What have you gained by him? He is a tyrant [just like] the others. You have only changed one tyrant for another, Louis for Napoleon." "*Mais, monsieur*, that may be; but, after all, he is the king of the *people*, and the Bourbons were the kings of the nobles. We have chosen *him*, and if we are to have a tyrant, let him be one chosen by ourselves." "There," said Napoleon, "you have the sentiments of the French nation expressed by an old woman."[46]

Napoleon may have been a man of the people, but his fall was caused by his own character flaws, most importantly his inability to rein in his ambition and to accept moral responsibility for his decisions, which resulted in the deaths of millions. Napoleon was at heart a soldier, one of the most brilliant military leaders in history. But he lacked the moral standards that would have prevented him from ordering endless, futile wars or undertaking diplomatic maneuvering that in the end brought nothing but misery to his adopted nation. As Gregor Dallas aptly describes him in *The Final Act: The Roads to Waterloo:*

> The Emperor was not a cold-hearted man; he was a man of passion, he enjoyed friendship, and he sincerely believed that his cause was good. Napoleon was not driven by unbridled ambition either; his acts were measured; he disciplined himself with reason, absolute reason. The people, he said, had put him in his position, and so in a sense they had: there was an angry, vengeful crowd behind Napoleon.

That perhaps was the problem. What Napoleon lacked most was a sense of what Europeans in the twentieth century—after two world wars—would call "collective responsibility." Napoleon either moved with the crowd or he repressed it; but he never thought for a moment that he and the crowd that moved with him were collectively responsible for the ap-

---

 ## Napoleon's Commanders Give Up

The incompetence of his generals proved to be a crucial reason for Napoleon's defeat at Waterloo. Ordinarily skilled and determined, Marshal Ney, for example, ordered foolish cavalry charges—or responded to orders with simple inaction. Ney, Grouchy, Jerome Bonaparte, and the other military commanders failed the emperor on this fateful battlefield, and the reason, according to historian Alan Schom in his book *Napoleon Bonaparte*, may have been simple battle fatigue on the part of the generals:

> Ney's puzzling inactivitiy on the morning of 16 June was to prove disastrous for the French. . . . Instead of ordering his troops forward, after a good breakfast, the marshal left the village at seven o'clock to inspect the situation at the forward outpost at Frasnes. "Ney's conduct on the morning of the 16th," admits Napoleonic expert General Camon, "Is absolutely incomprehensible." . . . In Ney's case there was of course the added element of his long-festering feud with [General Nicolas-Jean] Soult, especially since the Peninsular campaign. There also remained the simple fact that these commanders, *all of them*, were equally sick and tired of Napoleon Bonaparte and his madcap schemes.

---

*A nineteenth century painting portrays Napoleon reflecting on the shore of Saint Helena, a tiny island in the South Atlantic Ocean where he eventually died in 1821.*

palling acts they committed. . . . The idea that a nation, a society, or the movers of a revolution should accept responsibility for mass slaughter and economic catastrophe never crossed his mind.[47]

# Notes

## Chapter 1: The Failed Egyptian Campaign

1. Quoted in Felix Markham, *Napoleon and the Awakening of Europe*. New York: Collier Books, 1965, p. 27.
2. Quoted in Alan Schom, *Napoleon Bonaparte*. New York: HarperCollins, 1997, p. 63.
3. Quoted in Michael Glover, *The Napoleonic Wars: An Illustrated History, 1792–1815*. New York: Hippocrene Books, 1978, p. 50.
4. Jacques Bainville, *Napoleon*. Boston: Little, Brown and Co., 1933, p. 81.
5. Quoted in J. Christopher Herold, *The Age of Napoleon*. New York: Houghton Mifflin, 2002, p. 294.
6. Michael Broers, *Europe Under Napoleon, 1799–1815*. London: Arnold, 1996, p. 101.
7. Quoted in Maurice Hutt, ed., *Napoleon*. Englewood Cliffs, NJ: Prentice-Hall, 1972, pp. 105–106.

## Chapter 2: Failed Economics: The Continental System

8. Glover, *The Napoleonic Wars*, p. 128.
9. Quoted in Joe H. Kirchberger, *The French Revolution and Napoleon: An Eyewitness History*. New York: Facts On File, 1989, p. 331.
10. Herold, *The Age of Napoleon*, p. 243.
11. Bainville, *Napoleon*, p. 214.
12. Quoted in Broers, *Europe Under Napoleon, 1799–1815*, p. 147.

## Chapter 3: The Peninsular War: The Emperor Overreaches

13. Quoted in Glover, *The Napoleonic Wars*, p. 129.
14. James Marshall-Cornwall, *Napoleon as Military Commander*. New York: Barnes and Noble, 1998, p. 179.

15. Quoted in Frank A. Kafker and James M. Laux, eds., *Napoleon and His Times: Selected Interpretations*. Malabar, FL: Robert E. Krieger, 1989, p. 206.
16. Quoted in Glover, *The Napoleonic Wars*, p. 132.
17. Quoted in Kafker and Laux, *Napoleon and His Times*, p. 227.
18. Bainville, *Napoleon,* pp. 237–38.
19. Glover, *The Napoleonic Wars*, p. 144.
20. Quoted in Schom, *Napoleon Bonaparte*, p. 486.
21. Marshall-Cornwall, *Napoleon as Military Commander*, p. 180.

## Chapter 4: Underestimating the Enemy

22. Philip Longworth, *The Cossacks*. New York: Holt, Rinehart and Winston, 1969, p. 239.
23. Broers, *Europe Under Napoleon, 1799–1815*, p. 235.
24. Herold, *The Age of Napoleon*, p. 291.
25. Richard K. Riehn, *1812: Napoleon's Russian Campaign*. New York: McGraw-Hill, 1990, p. 407.
26. Broers, *Europe Under Napoleon, 1799–1815*, p. 235.
27. Quoted in Schom, *Napoleon Bonaparte*, p. 602.
28. Bainville, *Napoleon*, pp. 321–22.
29. Quoted in Kafker and Laux, *Napoleon and His Times*, p. 246.

## Chapter 5: Choosing the Sword: Defeat in Germany

30. Francois Furet, *Revolutionary France, 1770–1880*. Oxford, UK: Blackwell, 1995, p. 260.
31. Albert Sidney Britt III, *The Wars of Napoleon*. Wayne, NJ: Avery Publishing Group, 1985, p. 122.
32. Herold, *The Age of Napoleon*, p. 365.
33. Britt, *The Wars of Napoleon*, p. 122.
34. Britt, *The Wars of Napoleon*, p. 101.
35. Quoted in Marshall-Cornwall, *Napoleon as Military Commander*, p. 234.
36. Britt, *The Wars of Napoleon*, p. 142.
37. Furet, *Revolutionary France, 1770–1880*, p. 265.
38. Quoted in David Hamilton-Williams, *The Fall of Napoleon*. New York: John Wiley and Sons, 1994, p. 61.
39. Quoted in Britt, *The Wars of Napoleon*, p. 147.

## Chapter 6: A Failure of Perception: Defeat at Waterloo

40. Furet, *Revolutionary France, 1770–1880*, pp. 275–76.

41. Hamilton-Williams, *The Fall of Napoleon*, p. 201.
42. John Sutherland, *Men of Waterloo*. Englewood Cliffs, NJ: Prentice-Hall, 1967, pp. 53–54.
43. Marshall-Cornwall, *Napoleon as Military Commander*, p. 278.
44. Sutherland, *Men of Waterloo*, p. 250.
45. Quoted in Alan Schom, *One Hundred Days: Napoleon's Road to Waterloo*. New York: Oxford University Press, 1993, p. 293.
46. Quoted in Hutt, *Napoleon*, p. 36.
47. Gregor Dallas, *The Final Act: The Roads to Waterloo*. New York: Henry Holt and Co., 1996, pp. 271–72.

# Chronology

**1769**
Napoleon Bonaparte is born in Ajaccio, Corsica.

**1785**
Napoleon earns a commission as a second lieutenant of artillery.

**1789**
The French Revolution erupts as rioting and violence spread throughout the capital of Paris.

**1793**
Napoleon directs a bombardment of the French port of Toulon, driving out a British and Spanish fleet.

**1796**
Napoleon is appointed as the commander in chief of France's Army of Italy.

**1798**
Napoleon leads a military expedition to Egypt to strike a blow at the Ottoman and British Empires.

**1799**
After returning from Egypt, Napoleon overthrows the revolutionary government known as the Directory, then establishes himself as first consul.

**1800**
Napoleon scores a series of victories against the army of Austria in northern Italy.

**1801**
France makes peace with Austria by the Peace of Luneville, by which Austria acknowledges French dominance over northern Italy.

## 1802

France and England sign the Treaty of Amiens, in which England allows France control over important Caribbean colonies, and France agrees to evacuate Naples and the Papal States; by a plebiscite, Napoleon is named first consul for life.

## 1804

Napoleon crowns himself as emperor of France.

## 1805

Napoleon defeats the Austrian and Russian armies at the Battle of Austerlitz; the French navy is decisively defeated at the Battle of Trafalgar.

## 1806

By the Berlin Decree, Napoleon orders the confiscation of British goods and all ships found to be carrying British goods or trading with Britain.

## 1807

Napoleon and the Russian czar Alexander I sign the Treaty of Tilsit.

## 1808

French armies arrive in Spain to support the puppet monarchy of Joseph Bonaparte.

## 1812

Napoleon invades Russia in June, but is driven out after a miserable retreat from the capital of Moscow.

## 1813

Napoleon invades Germany to check the gathering army of the Allies, which defeats the French army at the Battle of Leipzig.

## 1814

The Allies invade France, capture Paris on March 30; Napoleon abdicates on April 7 and is escorted to the island of Elba.

## 1815

Napoleon escapes from Elba and returns to Paris to reestablish the empire; he is defeated in June at the Battle of Waterloo, then is exiled to the island of Saint Helena.

## 1821

Napoleon dies on Saint Helena.

# For Further Reading

Robert Asprey, *The Reign of Napoleon Bonaparte.* New York: Basic-Books, 2001. The second part of a two-part biography of Napoleon, using vivid detail and expert analysis to describe the emperor's military campaigns from 1805 to 1815.

Napoleon Bonaparte, *How to Make War.* New York: Ediciones La Calavera, 1998. A new translation of Napoleon's military maxims and memoirs, which first appeared in English in 1831.

Robert Gardiner, ed., *Nelson Against Napoleon: From the Nile to Copenhagen, 1798–1801.* Annapolis, MD: U.S. Naval Institute, 1997. A description of the English naval strategy in the early years of Napoleon's career that would play a vital role in the eventual defeat of the Napoleonic empire.

Paul Johnson, *Napoleon: A Penguin Life.* New York: Viking Press, 2002. A description of Napoleon's career, in which the author contends that in many ways Napoleon paved the way for the totalitarian states and world wars of the twentieth century.

Henry Lachouque, *The Anatomy of Glory: Napoleon and His Guard: A Study in Leadership.* London: Greenhill Books, 1997. A comprehensive and detailed reference work on Napoleon's elite and formidable Imperial Guard, written by the foremost French military historian of the Napoleonic era.

Frank McLynn, *Napoleon.* New York: Arcade Publishing, 2002. An overview of Napoleon's life and of Napoleonic Europe, offering a psychological analysis of Napoleon that brings insight into the public actions that resulted from Napoleon's private strengths, weaknesses, and idiosyncracies.

Claude-Francois Meneval and Proctor Patterson Jones, eds., *Napoleon: An Intimate Account of the Years of Supremacy: 1800–1814.* New York: Random House, 1992. An insider's account of Napoleon by two men who knew him, his secretary,

Meneval, and Constant, his personal valet; well illustrated with paintings and Napoleonic memorabilia.

Andrew Roberts, *Napoleon and Wellington: The Battle of Waterloo and the Great Commanders Who Fought It.* New York: Simon and Schuster, 2002. A study of the lives and characters of the two main adversaries at Waterloo, concentrating on the relationship between the two men and pointing out the similarities in their lives as well as the important differences in their characters.

# Works Consulted

Jacques Bainville, *Napoleon*. Boston: Little, Brown and Co., 1933. A French biography that delves into the motives behind Napoleon's actions and attempts to describe and define the emperor's true character.

Albert Sidney Britt III, *The Wars of Napoleon*. Wayne, NJ: Avery Publishing Group, 1985. A technical manual for army cadets that goes into great detail on the major Napoleonic battles and the overall strategy that governed Napoleon's campaigns.

Michael Broers, *Europe Under Napoleon, 1799–1815*. London: Arnold, 1996. A description of ordinary life in Europe during the Napoleonic era and the social, political, and economic consequences of Napoleon's conquests and the imposition of his empire in Europe.

Gregor Dallas, *The Final Act: The Roads to Waterloo*. New York: Henry Holt and Co., 1996. A detailed account of the diplomatic maneuvers at the Congress of Vienna and of Napoleon's final campaign against the Allies, which ended in his final defeat.

Denis Davidov, *In the Service of the Tsar Against Napoleon: The Memoirs of Denis Davidov, 1806–1814*. London: Greenhill Books, 1999. A memoir of a Russian officer who experienced firsthand Napoleon's Russian campaign in the summer and fall of 1812.

David L. Dowd, *Napoleon: Was He the Heir of the Revolution?* New York: Holt, Rinehart and Winston, 1964. A review of the debate among historians over Napoleon's true origins in revolutionary France and his ultimate legacy in the radically changed France that he left behind.

Francois Furet, *Revolutionary France, 1770–1880*. Oxford, UK: Blackwell, 1995. A book covering the social and political background and consequences of the French Revolution, from the last years of the Bourbon monarchy to the late nineteenth century.

Michael Glover, *The Napoleonic Wars: An Illustrated History, 1792–1815*. New York: Hippocrene Books, 1978. An introduction to the military and diplomatic aspects of Napoleon's campaigns.

David Hamilton-Williams, *The Fall of Napoleon*. New York: John Wiley and Sons, 1994. A study of Napoleon's fall from power—concluding that it was mainly self-inflicted—and the coordinated efforts of Allied diplomats to bring an end to Napoleon's reign in Europe.

J. Christopher Herold, *The Age of Napoleon*. New York: Houghton Mifflin, 2002. An updated biography of Napoleon, giving detailed background on the political and economic life of Europe in the late eighteenth and early nineteenth centuries.

John Eldred Howard, ed., *Letters and Documents of Napoleon*. London: Cresset Press, 1961. A collection of Napoleon's writings that lends important insight into his character and motives, although the reader and student must beware of the emperor's great skill at propaganda and self-advertisement.

Maurice Hutt, ed., *Napoleon*. Englewood Cliffs, NJ: Prentice-Hall, 1972. A collection of the diaries, letters, and memoirs of people who personally knew or encountered Napoleon.

Frank A. Kafker and James M. Laux, eds., *Napoleon and His Times: Selected Interpretations*. Malabar, FL: Robert E. Krieger, 1989. Essays on the Napoleonic era, illustrating the lively debate that has been taking place among students of the period over Napoleon's impact on France and the rest of Europe.

Joe H. Kirchberger, *The French Revolution and Napoleon: An Eyewitness History*. New York: Facts On File, 1989. A reference book giving general background on the period and contemporary journals, letters, newspapers, and eyewitness accounts.

Philip Longworth, *The Cossacks*. New York: Holt, Rinehart and Winston, 1969. A book about the tribesmen of the plains of Ukraine, who formed a semi-independent state and gained a reputation as the best cavalry fighters of Europe.

Felix Markham, *Napoleon and the Awakening of Europe*. New York: Collier Books, 1965. A general and now dated study of Napoleonic Europe.

James Marshall-Cornwall, *Napoleon as Military Commander*. New York: Barnes and Noble, 1998. An analysis of Napoleon's tactics on the battlefield, from his early Italian campaigns to Waterloo, and his handling of his officers and troops.

Richard K. Riehn, *1812: Napoleon's Russian Campaign*. New York: McGraw-Hill, 1990. The grim story of Napoleon's disastrous attack on Russia, a campaign that ended in the near-annihilation of the French army. The author concludes that faulty planning and indecision on the part of Napoleon were more responsible for the defeat than cold weather or Russian tenacity.

Alan Schom, *Napoleon Bonaparte*. New York: HarperCollins, 1997. A recent, detailed, and authoritative book on Napoleon's life and career by a noted scholar of the period.

———*One Hundred Days: Napoleon's Road to Waterloo*. New York: Oxford University Press, 1993. An account of Napoleon's escape from Elba, his entry into Paris, and his final campaign and defeat at Waterloo; the author points out that the battle might have been won but for the inaction and incompetence of Napoleon's generals and aides.

John Sutherland, *Men of Waterloo*. Englewood Cliffs, NJ: Prentice-Hall, 1967. A blow-by-blow description of the three-day Battle of Waterloo, which put a permanent end to Napoleon's mastery of France.

# Index

# Picture Credits

# About the Author

Thomas Streissguth is a critically acclaimed author of nonfiction books in the fields of history, geography, biography, and current events. He has written juvenile books for all grade levels and has also produced reference and nonfiction work for adults. He has traveled widely in Europe and the Middle East and has worked as a teacher, journalist, and editor. He is currently researching an historical novel set in antebellum New Orleans.